雙雙中文教材（20）
Chinese Language and Culture Course

中國歷史（下）*History of China (II)*

王雙雙 編著

北京大學出版社
PEKING UNIVERSITY PRESS

圖書在版編目（CIP）數據

中國歷史：繁體版.下／（美）王雙雙編著.—北京：北京大學出版社，2009.1
（雙雙中文教材20）
ISBN 978-7-301-14415-2

I.中… II.王… III.①漢語－對外漢語教學－教材 ②中國–通史 IV.H195.4

中國版本圖書館CIP數據核字（2008）第168382號

書　　名：中國歷史（下）
著作責任者：王雙雙 編著
英文翻譯：王亦兵
責任編輯：孫 嫻
標準書號：ISBN 978-7-301-14415-2/H・2100
出版發行：北京大學出版社
地　　址：北京市海淀區成府路205號 100871
網　　址：http://www.pup.cn
電　　話：郵購部 62752015 發行部 62750672 編輯部 62752028 出版部 62754962
電子信箱：zpup@pup.pku.edu.cn
印 刷 者：北京大學印刷廠
經 銷 者：新華書店
889毫米×1194毫米 16開本 11印張 163千字
2009年1月第1版 2009年1月第1次印刷
定　　價：100.00元（含課本、練習册和CD-ROM一張）

前言

《雙雙中文教材》是一套專門為海外青少年編寫的中文課本，是我在美國八年的中文教學實踐基礎上編寫成的。在介紹這套教材之前，請讀一首小詩：

一雙神奇的手，

推開一扇窗。

一條神奇的路，

通向燦爛的中華文化。

鮑凱文　鮑維江

1998年

鮑維江和鮑凱文姐弟倆是美國生美國長的孩子，也是我的學生。1998年冬，他們送給我的新年賀卡上的小詩，深深地打動了我的心。我把這首詩看成我文化教學的"回聲"。我要傳達給海外每位中文老師：我教給他們（學生）中國文化，他們思考了、接受了、回應了。這條路走通了！

語言是交際的工具，更是一種文化和一種生活方式，所以學習中文也就離不開中華文化的學習。漢字是一種古老的象形文字，她從遠古走來，帶有大量的文化信息，但學起來並不容易。使學生增強興趣、減小難度，走出苦學漢字的怪圈，走進領悟中華文化的花園，是我編寫這套教材的初衷。

學生不論大小，天生都有求知的慾望，都有欣賞文化美的追求。中華文化本身是魅力十足的。把這宏大而玄妙的文化，深入淺出地，有聲有色地介紹出來，讓這迷人的文化如涓涓細流，一點一滴地滲入學生們的心田，使學生們逐步體味中國文化，是我編寫這套教材的目的。

為此我將漢字的學習放入文化介紹的流程之中同步進行，讓同學們在學中國地理的同時，學習漢字；在學中國歷史的同時，學習漢字；在學中國哲學的同時，學習漢字；在學中國科普文選的同時，學習漢字……

這樣的一種中文學習，知識性強，趣味性強；老師易教，學生易學。當學生們合上書本時，他們的眼前是中國的大好河山，是中國五千年的歷史和妙不可言的哲學思維，是奔騰的現代中國……

總之，他們瞭解了中華文化，就會探索這片土地，熱愛這片土地，就會與中國結下情緣。

最後我要衷心地感謝所有熱情支持和幫助我編寫教材的老師、家長、學生、朋友和家人，特別是老同學唐玲教授、何茜老師、我姐姐王欣欣編審和她的兒子楊眉及我女兒Uta Guo年復一年的鼎力相助。可以説這套教材是大家努力的結果。

王雙雙

説 明

《雙雙中文教材》是一套專門為海外學生編寫的中文教材。它是由美國加州王雙雙老師和中國專家學者共同努力，在海外多年的實踐中編寫出來的。全書共20册，識字量2500個，包括了從識字、拼音、句型、短文的學習，到初步的較系統的中國文化的學習。教材大體介紹了中國地理、歷史、哲學等方面的豐富內容，突出了中國文化的魅力。課本知識面廣，趣味性强，深入淺出，易教易學。

這套教材體系完整、構架靈活、使用面廣。學生可以從零起點開始，一直學完全部課程20册；也可以將後11册（10～20册）的九個文化專題和第五册（漢語拼音）單獨使用，這樣便於開設中國哲學、地理、歷史等專門課程以及假期班、短期中國文化班、拼音速成班的高中和大學使用，符合美國AP中文課程的目標和基本要求。

本書是《雙雙中文教材》的第二十册，由王雙雙在楊東梁先生（中國人民大學圖書館館長）的指導和幫助之下，在海外中文教學實踐的基礎上編寫而成。全書語言簡單，概要地介紹了中國從唐代下半葉到清代末期的歷史知識。學生們通過學習，不僅能較系統地瞭解中國歷史，中文的識字數量和語匯水平也將得到明顯的提高。

考慮到海外漢語歷史教學的特殊性，為了便利教學，本書的編寫采取了化繁為簡的原則，歷史年代表中没有以王朝興起的年代為它的起始年代，而是以它正式替代前朝的時間為準，如：秦、清等朝；或者以正式設立本國號的年代為準，如：遼、元等朝。特此説明。

編者

課程設置

一年級	中文課本（第一册）	中文課本（第二册）	中文課本（第三册）
二年級	中文課本（第四册）	中文課本（第五册）	中文課本（第六册）
三年級	中文課本（第七册）	中文課本（第八册）	中文課本（第九册）
四年級	中國成語故事	中國地理常識	
五年級	中國古代故事	中國神話傳説	
六年級	中國古代科學技術	中國文學欣賞	
七年級	中國詩歌欣賞	中文科普閱讀	
八年級	中國古代哲學	中國歷史（上）	
九年級	中國歷史（下）	小説閱讀，中文SAT Ⅱ	
十年級	中文SAT Ⅱ（強化班）	小説閱讀，中文SAT Ⅱ考試	

目　錄

第十一課　唐（下）……………………………… 1

第十二課　五代十國和北宋 ……………………… 14

第十三課　遼、西夏、金與南宋……………… 26

第十四課　成吉思汗和他的子孫…………… 38

第十五課　元 ………………………………… 46

第十六課　明（上）…………………………… 58

第十七課　明（下）…………………………… 71

第十八課　清（上）…………………………… 80

第十九課　清（下）…………………………… 91

生字表　…………………………………… 102

生詞表　…………………………………… 104

中國歷史朝代年表 ………………………… 108

第十一課

唐（下）

唐朝建立之後，一直蓬勃發展。從唐太宗到唐玄宗統治前期的一百多年間是唐朝的全盛時期。這時的唐朝政治安定，經濟繁榮，文化發達，軍力強大，是當時世界上最富庶、最強盛的國家。

安史之亂

唐玄宗統治後期，生活奢侈，皇宮裏專門織錦、刺繡的工匠就有700人。唐玄宗寵愛楊貴妃，不再關心國家的事情。他任用楊貴妃的堂兄楊國忠為宰相，國家混亂、腐敗。

公元755年，軍閥安祿山與部將史思明起兵反唐，佔領長安，史稱“安史之亂”。唐玄宗倉皇逃往四川。走到半路，憤怒的將士們殺死了楊國忠，並要求皇帝把楊貴妃處(chǔ)死。唐玄宗無奈，只好讓人處死了楊貴妃。

唐代貴族銅鏡（鑲黃金飛鳥和白銀花朵）

後來太子繼帝位，史稱唐肅宗。唐軍經過八年戰鬥，最後平

定了叛亂。安史之亂使人民無家可歸，田地荒蕪，唐朝從此由強盛走向衰落。

唐中期以後，均田制被破壞，許多大官佔有良田萬畝，而失地的農民越來越多，他們生活日益困苦，不斷起來反抗。

唐朝末年爆發了黃巢起義，義軍兵力達10餘萬人。起義軍轉戰大半個中國，最後攻佔了長安，黃巢稱帝，國號“大齊”。但是起義軍將領朱溫叛變，黃巢被唐軍打敗，退出長安，後來在泰山附近兵敗自殺。

黃巢起義失敗後，各地軍隊將領的勢力更大。公元907年，武將朱溫政變成功，建立梁朝，建國290年的唐帝國滅亡。

燦爛的隋唐文化

隋唐時期，是中國經濟文化繁榮開放的時期。隋唐政府積極同各國交往，當時與中國通商的國家有70多個。長安不僅是唐朝的首都，也是當時世界的一個中心。來自新羅（朝鮮）、日本、波斯和東羅馬等國的幾千名外國商人和留學生雲集在長安、洛陽、廣州等城市。唐朝政府平等對待他們，允許

樂舞壁畫（唐）

波斯人物白玉帶板（唐）

他們長期在中國居住、和中國人通婚甚至在中國當官。在長安、洛陽這些大城市，有許多外國商人開的商店和酒館，其中西域商人開的商店最多。在那裏，人們可以吃到胡人①的美味食品，欣賞胡人的優美樂舞。唐代胡人多彩的服飾也深受漢族婦女的喜愛。那時，朝鮮音樂也受到中國人的廣泛歡迎。這一時期，漢族有機會和其他民族生活在一起，各族文化相互交流，使漢族吸收了不少外來的文化，在科技、宗教、文學藝術等方面都有新的發展，創造了燦爛的隋唐文化。隋唐文化是中國古代文化的高峰，也走在當時世界文化發展的前列。

大雁塔

隋唐時期各地大量興建宮殿、寺廟、佛塔和住宅。唐朝的都城長安是當時世界上最大的城市之一。城市為長方形，外圍城牆②周長36.7千米。城中五條主要街道寬百米以上。大明宮是長安最宏偉氣派的建築。隋唐時期其他著名的建築

① 胡人——古代泛稱中國北方和西方的其他民族。

② 中國古代在城的外圍加築一道外城牆。

還有：河北趙縣的趙州橋、陝西西安的大雁塔等。

在隋唐時期，佛教、道教得到極大傳播。景教[①]、伊斯蘭教也傳入中國。唐太宗允許景教徒在長安建寺，伊斯蘭教徒建立清真寺。這些外來的宗教，對中國的建築、雕刻、繪畫都有很大的影響。

《金剛經》局部（唐）

在天文學方面，唐玄宗時，天文學家一行和尚測量出了子午線的長度。這是世界上最早測量子午線的記錄。醫學上，孫思邈著有《千金方》等書籍。書中收集了各種藥方，總結了寶貴的醫療經驗。隋唐時期，還發明了雕版印刷術，現在世界上最早的雕版印刷品《金剛經》就是唐朝印製的。

唐朝是中國詩歌的黄金時代，至今已收集了近50,000首唐代詩歌，作者達2,000多人。著名詩人有李白、杜甫和白居易等。

簪花仕女圖（唐・周昉）

① 景教——基督教的一支。它的教義融合了波斯文化的內容，傳入中國後又吸收了佛教、道教和儒家的思想。

唐朝的繪畫和書法的成就也很高。著名畫家吳道子有"畫聖"之稱；在書法藝術方面，歐陽詢的"歐體"、顏真卿(qīng)的"顏體"、柳公權的"柳體"風格各不相同，對後世影響很大。

生詞

péng bó 蓬勃	vigorous; flourishing		pàn biàn 叛變	rebell; betray (one's country)
fù shù 富庶	rich and prosperous		càn làn 燦爛	splendid; resplendent
cì xiù 刺繡	embroidery		yǔn xǔ 允許	permit; allow
chǒng ài 寵愛	favor; dote on		zōng jiào 宗教	religion
guì fēi 貴妃	highest-ranking imperial concubine		zǐ wǔ xiàn 子午線	meridian
fèn nù 憤怒	angry; furious		ōu yáng xún 歐陽詢	Ouyang Xun (*name*) 詢:inquire
wú nài 無奈	have no way out		fēng gé 風格	style
huáng cháo 黃巢	Huang Chao (*name*)			

聽寫

蓬勃　寵愛　憤怒　無奈　叛變　燦爛　允許　宗教

風格　留學生　*富庶

注: *以後的字詞為選做題，後同。

比一比

叛	叛變	勃(蓬勃)	奈(無奈)	允(允許)
	叛亂	脖(脖子)	耐(忍耐)	充(充分)
宗	宗教	繡(刺繡)	爛(燦爛)	憤(憤怒)
	祖宗	肅(嚴肅)	欄(欄目)	噴(噴泉)

詞語運用

憤怒

示威的人們憤怒地喊著:“要和平,不要戰爭!”

無奈

周末準備去爬山,無奈天下雨,去不成了。

允許

請大家注意,這裏不允許抽煙。

多音字

chǔ 處	chù 處
chǔ 處死	chù 到處

回答問題

1. 為什麼説唐朝是中國歷史上很開放的時期？那時有多少國家與唐通商？

2. 唐代，漢族和其他民族生活在一起，對文化的發展有什麼好處？

3. 請説一説隋唐時期有哪些著名建築。

4. 唐代有哪些科學技術和文化藝術成就？

詞語解釋

堂兄——父親之間是兄弟，他們的兒子互稱堂兄弟，年長的為堂兄。

倉皇——急忙而慌張。

處死——給予死刑處罰。

叛亂——武裝叛變。

留學生——留居外國讀書的學生。

雲集——比喻很多人從各處來，聚集在一起。

平等——指人們在社會、政治、經濟、法律等各方面受到同等對待。

閱讀

敦煌莫高窟

莫高窟，俗稱千佛洞，位於甘肅省河西走廊西端，敦煌市東南，在鳴沙山東麓50多米高的崖壁上，洞窟層層排列。

公元366年（前秦），一位名叫樂尊的僧人雲游到此，因看到三危山金光萬道，感到這裏一定是佛地，便在崖壁上開鑿了第一個佛窟。以後經過一代一代的修建，現在保存有北涼至元代的洞窟700多個，壁畫5萬多平方米，彩塑2,700多尊。

飛天

敦煌莫高窟的洞窟十之六七是隋唐時期開鑿的，其中壁畫內容表現了佛教故事，不少畫面也反映了隋唐時期社會的繁榮。有帝王、貴族、官吏的豪華生活，有西域各族人民的形象，有中外商人貿易的情景，有農夫耕田、漁夫打魚、船工背縴、工匠營造等勞動場面。壁畫的色彩絢麗奪目，形象生動。其中，身披飄拂長帶、在長空飛舞的“飛天”和“反彈琵琶”、載歌載舞的仙女，是敦煌壁畫的代表作。

飛天

莫高窟的塑像，有的沉思，有的微笑，有的威嚴，有的勇猛，個個神情逼真，富於藝術魅力。最大的佛像高33米。著名作家余秋雨曾寫到：“看莫高窟，不是看死了一千年的標本，而是看活了一千年的生命。”莫高窟是一座文化藝術的寶庫。

反彈琵琶

生詞

dūn huáng 敦煌	Dunhuang (*place*)		piāo fú 飄拂	drift slightly
shān lù 山麓	foot of a mountain		fǎn tán 反彈	play (a lute) on one's back
yá bì 崖壁	cliff; precipice		pí pá 琵琶	lute
háo huá 豪華	luxurious; extravagant		sù xiàng 塑像	sculpture
bēi qiàn 背縴	tow		chén sī 沉思	ponder
yíng zào 營造	construct; build		bī zhēn 逼真	lifelike
xuàn lì duó mù 絢麗奪目	magnificent; bright and colorful		mèi lì 魅力	charm
pī 披	wear		biāo běn 標本	specimen; sample

English Translation

Lesson 11

Tang (II)

The Tang Dynasty flourished for a long time and was at its peak for more than 100 years starting from the reign of Emperor Taizong to Emperor Xuanzong. During this period of time, Tang was the richest and most prosperous country in the world. It was politically stable, culturally developed, and had a powerful military force.

The An-Shi Rebellion

During the later part of his reign, Emperor Xuanzong of the Tang Dynasty lived an extremely luxurious life. A demonstration of the kind of life lived by the imperial family is seen in the instance of the hiring of 700 silk weavers and embroiderers to serve only them in the palace. He favored Lady Yang most and didn't care about national affairs. He appointed Yang Guozhong, the cousin of Lady Yang, as his Prime Minister to manage the country in his stead. This led to disorder and corruption in the entire country.

In A.D. 755, warlord An Lushan and his officer Shi Siming rebelled against Tang and captured the capital city, Chang'an. This is known in history as the An-Shi Rebellion. Emperor Xuanzong fled in a hurry to Sichuan. Halfway through their escape route, angry generals and soldiers killed Yang Guozhong and forced the emperor to put Lady Yang to death. Emperor Xuanzong could do nothing else but to have Lady Yang killed.

The crown prince then succeeded the throne and became Emperor Suzong of the Tang Dynasty. The rebellion was finally suppressed and put down after eight years of military effort. During the period of the An-Shi Rebellion, a lot of people became homeless and this led to the fields being neglected and deserted, with no one to harvest the crops. Because of this, the Tang Dynasty started to decline.

After the Mid-Tang Dynasty, the land-equalization system was destroyed, and officials and officers occupied large amounts of fertile fields which led to farmers losing more and more land. They became increasingly poor and were forced to rise up and rebel for their rights.

At the end of the Tang Dynasty, the Huang Chao Uprising broke out and there were more than 100,000 soldiers involved in the rebellion. They swept through most places in China and finally took over Chang'an. Huang Chao came to the throne and named the country Da Qi. Later on, due to the betrayal of his own general Zhu Wen, Huang Chao was defeated by Tang and retreated from the capital city before losing the final battle around Mount Tai and committed suicide.

After the failure of the Huang Chao Uprising, the local military generals enjoyed more power. In A.D. 907, General Zhu Wen launched a successful coup d'état and founded the Liang Dynasty. The great Tang Empire with a history of 290 years came to an end.

The Splendid Cultures in the Sui and Tang Dynasties

The economy and Chinese culture flourished during the Sui and Tang Dynasties. The government communicated actively with foreign countries and more than 70 countries enjoyed trade relations with China at that time. Chang'an was not only the capital city of the Tang Dynasty, but also a world trade center. Thousands of foreign businessmen and students from Korea, Japan, Persia, and the Eastern Roman empire gathered in Chang'an, Luoyang, and Guangzhou. The Tang government treated all of them equally and allowed them to stay in China for a long time, and they could marry the Chinese locals or become officials in China. In major cities like Chang'an and Luoyang, there were many stores and restaurants operated by foreign businessmen, especially those that businessmen from the Western Regions invested in. Local people could enjoy the delicious food and the beautiful music and dancing of the Western Regions in these stores and restaurants. The colorful costumes of the Western Regions were also favored by women of the Han nationality, and Korean music was extensively popular in China. During that time, people of the Han nationality lived together with other nationalities. Due to cultural exchanges and communications with these people, the Han nationality group absorbed a lot of foreign culture, and this led to great progress in technology, religion, literature, and art, creating the splendid Sui and Tang culture. Ancient Chinese culture reached its peak during Sui and Tang Dynasties and also in the rest of the world.

A large amount of palaces, temples, pagodas and residential buildings were built during the Sui and Tang Dynasties, and the capital city of the Tang Dynasty, Chang'an, used to be one of the biggest cities in the world at that time. The city was shaped like a rectangle and the total length of its outer wall was 36.7 km. There were five main streets that were each more than 100 meters wide, and the Daming Palace was the most magnificent construction in Chang'an. Other famous architectural works during Sui and Tang Dynastyies include the Zhaozhou Bridge in County Zhao, Hebei Province, and the Big Wild Goose Pagoda in Xi'an, Shaanxi Province.

Both Buddhism and Taoism flourished during Sui and Tang Dynasties. Other religions and belief systems such as Nestorianism and Islamism were also introduced into China. Emperor Taizong of the Tang Dynasty allowed both Christians and Moslems to build a church and a mosque in Chang'an too. These foreign religions contributed a great deal to Chinese architecture, sculpture art, and painting.

During the reign of Emperor Xuanzong of the Tang Dynasty, the astronomy field saw some developments as well. Master Yixing, a monk and astronomer, measured the length of the meridian, and this is the earliest record of the measurement of the meridian in the world. In the medical science field, Sun Simiao collected different prescriptions and summarized precious medical experiences in his famous book entitled *Prescriptions Worth a Thousand Gold*. The engraving typography was invented during the Sui and Tang Dynasties and the earliest existing engraved work in the world, *Diamond Sutra*, was printed during the Tang Dynasty.

The Tang Dynasty is also known as the Golden Age of poetry in China and there are nearly 50,000 poems composed by more than 2,000 poets which includes famous names as Li Bai, Du Fu, and Bai Juyi handed down from then to today.

The achievements of painting and calligraphy were also significant in the Tang Dynasty. The prestigious painter Wu Daozi was famed as the "saint painter", and in the field of calligraphy, the Ou style of Ouyang Xun, the Yan style of Yan Zhenqing, and the Liu style of Liu Gongquan have profound influence on all calligraphy writers till today.

The Dunhuang Mogao Grottoes

Mogao Grottoes, also known as the Thousand Buddha Grottoes, are located on the west end of the Hexi Corridor in the Gansu Province to the southeast of Dunhuang City and on a 50 meter high cliff on the east slope of the Mingsha Mountain. These grottoes are arranged in layers.

In A.D. 366 (during the Qianqin period), a monk named Le Zun was on his travels when he saw numerous golden rays radiating from the Sanwei Mountain. Believing this must be a shrine, he carved the first grotto on the cliff. After many generations of construction, there were more than 700 grottos that can be dated back to the Kingdom of Northern Liang till the Yuan Dynasty, with murals that reach up to 50,000 square meters and more than 2,700 painted sculptures.

About 60 to 70 percent of the Dunhuang Mogao Grottoes were constructed during the Sui and Tang Dynasties. The murals depicted Buddhist stories and the prosperity that people enjoyed during that time. Many murals were about the luxurious lives lived by emperors, noblemen, officials, as well as images of different peoples in the Western Regions, the trading scenes of domestic and foreign businessmen, the working scenes of farmers plowing fields, fishermen catching fish, boatmen towing boats, and craftsmen working on their artwork. These murals are splendidly colorful and the images are vividly depicted. Among them was a picture that depicted a flying goddess with long waving rib-

bons that danced in the sky, and another shows a dancing fairy playing a lute on her back. These are masterworks representing the art of Dunhuang murals.

The sculptures of the Mogao Grottoes are true to life and full of artistic charms. Some depict people meditating, some depict people smiling, and others may depict notions of bravery and courage. The largest Buddha statue is 33 meters high. According to Yu Qiuyu, a famous Chinese writer, who said, "When you look at the Mogao Grottoes, you're looking at a thousand years of life instead of a thousand years of death." The Mogao Grottoes are indeed treasuries of culture and art.

第十二課

五代十國和北宋

唐朝滅亡後，中國又分裂成很多小國。在五十多年的時間裏，五個大國先後統治了黄河一帶，史稱後梁、後唐、後晋、後漢、後周，合稱“五代”。同一時期，在中國的南方各地先後建立了吴、南唐、楚等九個國家，加上山西一帶的北漢，史稱“十國”①。

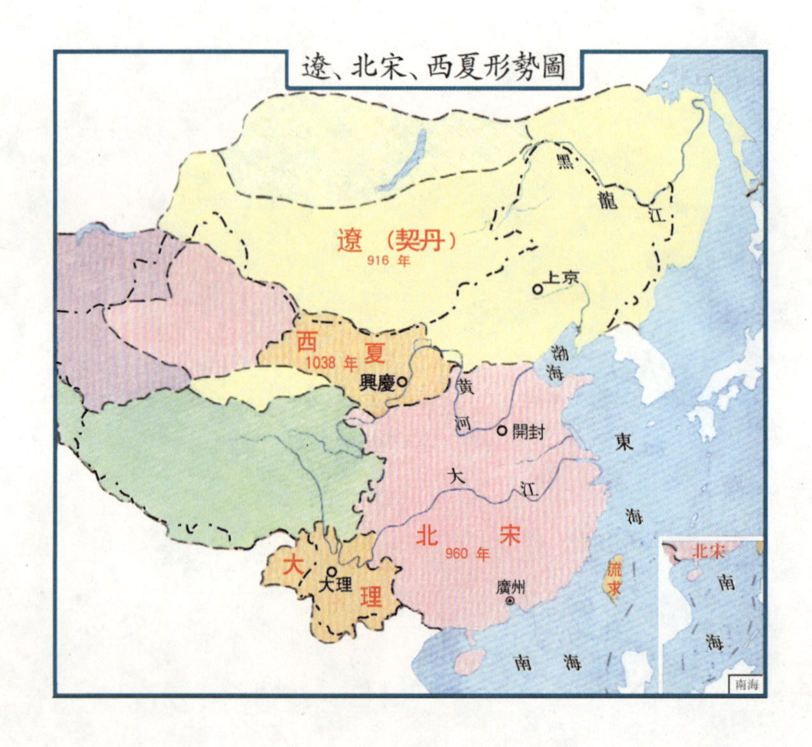

公元960年，趙匡胤（kuāng yìn）奪取後周皇帝的政權，建立宋朝，史稱北宋，首都是開封。公元979年，北宋統一全國，結束了五代十國的分裂局面。

北宋建國後，宋

① 歷史上把這一時期總稱為“五代十國”。

太祖趙匡胤吸取了五代十國軍閥分裂國家的教訓，他不願意再看見軍人威脅君主，於是在一次酒宴上解除了將軍們的兵權，由皇帝直接控制軍隊。他還建立了一套文官制度來管理國家，重文輕武的傳統開始了。宋朝的科舉制較為嚴格。經過科舉，許多出身低微但有才能的人被選拔出來成為官員，而没有真才實學的人很難考上。宋朝的科舉制使政府得到了很多人才，但是也漸漸形成了“萬般皆下品，唯有讀書高”的社會價值觀念。

北宋中期，土地集中的現象很嚴重，全國一半農民没有土地，農民不斷起義。由於對遼、西夏戰爭的失敗，宋朝不但割讓了土地，每年還要向遼、西夏交納歲幣，而養活軍隊和衆多官員所需要的開支又很龐大，政府財政十分困難。面對嚴重的政治、社會危機，改革家王安石在皇帝的支持下於公元1069年開始變法。變法內容一是理財，二是整軍。理財的辦法是：國家向農民低息貸款，興修水利，重新丈量土地，使稅收合理。整軍的辦法是：減少軍隊數量，加強軍隊的戰鬥力。但是，王安石推行的新法因受到保守派激烈的反對而失敗。

聽琴圖（宋徽宗）

北宋末年的皇帝宋徽宗，人稱“書畫皇帝”。他雖然在書畫上有超人的才華，喜愛花、石、竹、木，在京城大造園林，可是治理國家，他卻昏庸無能，任用奸臣，使宋末的政治十分黑暗。

與此同時，北方的女真族建立了金國。金國迅速強大起來，並於公元1125年消滅了遼國。就在滅遼的同一年，金國又出兵攻打宋。面對金兵的進攻，宋徽宗無力抵抗，將皇位讓給太子（也就是後來的宋欽宗）。此時，北宋軍隊在抗金將領李綱的指揮下，擊退了金軍。但由於宋徽宗和宋欽宗的無能，一心想與金國求和，他們罷免了李綱，又答應向金國割地賠款，金軍纔退走。公元1127年，金軍再次南下，攻佔了開封，並擄走宋徽宗、宋欽宗以及皇後、妃子、大臣3,000多人和大量財物，北宋滅亡。

北宋時，雖然北方戰亂不斷，但是南方比較安寧，因此科學技術有明顯的進步，例如：中國四大發明之一的活字印刷術出現；又由於戰爭的需要，火藥被首次應用於軍事。宋在文學藝術方面也達到了極

猛油火櫃——宋朝的火焰噴射器

高的水平。宋詞與唐詩並稱為中國古典文學藝術的瑰寶。在繪畫、書法藝術上，著名畫家張擇端的《清明上河圖》描繪了汴(biàn)京（開封）清明節的情景，畫面上共有將近600個人物，成為中國繪畫史上一幅不朽的作品。

生詞

jiě chú 解除	remove; disarm	jiān chén 奸臣	treacherous court official
jiāo nà 交納	pay; hand in	sòng qīn zōng 宋欽宗	Emperor Qinzong of Song Dynasty
cái zhèng 財政	finance	gē dì 割地	cede territory
gǎi gé 改革	reform	lǔ zǒu 擄走	capture
dī (lì) xī 低（利）息	low interest	guī bǎo 瑰寶	gem; treasure
bǎo shǒu pài 保守派	conservative	miáo huì 描繪	describe
hūn yōng 昏庸	fatuous	bù xiǔ 不朽	immortal; enduring

聽寫

財政　交納　改革　利息　描繪　割地　瑰寶　解除

不朽　稅收　*奸臣

比一比

息 { 利息 / 休息

財 { 財政 / 財産

税 { 税收 / 納税

描 { 描繪 / 掃描

割 { 割斷 / 割地

寶 { 瑰寶 / 珠寶

{ 朽（不朽） / 巧（花言巧語）

詞語運用

結束

節日慶祝活動在人們的歌聲、掌聲和歡笑聲中結束了。

不朽

這些英雄們建立了不朽的功勛。

回答問題

1. 請説一説王安石變法的主要内容是什麽。

2. “萬般皆下品，唯有讀書高”的觀念和科舉制有没有關係?

3. “宋詞與唐詩並稱為中國古典文學藝術的瑰寶”這句話對嗎?

詞語解釋

酒宴——請人一起飲酒吃飯的聚會（指比較隆重的）。

稅收——政府徵稅得到的收入。

罷免——免去官職。

賠款——戰敗國向戰勝國賠償(cháng)損失和作戰的費用。

首次——第一次。

閱讀

繁華的城鎮

北宋時，雖然北方與遼國常有戰爭，但中原和南方人民的生活還是安定和富足的。宋朝商業發達，是當時世界上的商業大國。

宋代，由於商業和手工業的發展，在一些港口和交通要道出現了許多大大小小的城鎮，形成了一個巨大的商業交換網。比如：有的城鎮以生產紙和鞋為主，有的城鎮印刷業很發達，有的城鎮以編竹籃和竹席出名……城鎮間不斷進行商品交換，帶動了交通的發展。那時城鎮裏出現了大量的流動人口，客店、酒樓、茶館、店鋪一家挨著一家，城鎮裏生機勃勃。

北宋的都城汴京，是當時世界上著名的大城市，有居民20萬戶。城內大街小巷有數不清的店鋪、酒樓、飯館，一直營業到深夜。還有“瓦肆”，是娛樂場所，那裏有戲曲、雜技和武術表演。城裏的夜市很熱鬧。天還沒亮，早市又活躍起來，人來人往，非常繁華。著名的《清明上河圖》，就清楚地再現了宋朝的城市生活。

清明上河圖

《清明上河圖》是宋朝畫家張擇端的作品。這幅畫作在中國歷史上非常著名。張擇端是北宋人，他年輕的時候生活在北宋的首都汴京。他學習繪畫，特別喜歡畫房屋、城市、車船、河流、道路等等。

北宋滅亡後，許多人逃到南方，張擇端也來到南方。回想起以前在汴京清明時節，汴河兩岸的風光和人物，他十分懷念。於是他就憑著自己的記憶，把汴京各種繁華熱鬧的情景都一一畫了出來，畫成了一幅長長的畫卷（全長5.25米，高0.255米）。

這畫畫得太好了，畫的是汴京真實生活的情景。畫上有汴河兩岸的農田、道路和河上的橋，還有河中運糧運貨的大船、小船。碼頭上人們不停地忙著裝貨、卸貨。商隊的駱駝、馬車來來往往。路邊、橋上，到處是商店，賣糧的、賣肉的、賣水

《清明上河圖》局部二幅（宋・張擇端）

果的，還有算命的鋪子……畫家把汴河邊商業區的熱鬧景象全都畫出來了。

再看畫面上的人物，街上有抬著花轎的迎親隊伍，有圍著戲臺看戲的人群，有觀看和尚武術表演的大人和孩子，有在茶館與朋友喝茶閑聊的人。再看看宮牆裏面，皇后正由宮女扶著上龍船準備遊湖……一切畫得是那麼生動、詳細。

當你看這幅畫的時候，就像你正在沿著汴河河岸行走，親眼看到宋朝熱鬧的街市以及宮廷和平民的生活情景。這是一幅難得的歷史藝術畫卷。

生詞

diàn pù 店鋪	shop	xì qǔ 戲曲	traditional opera
shēng jī bó bó 生機勃勃	dynamic; full of vitality	zá jì 雜技	acrobatics
biànjīng 汴京	Bianjing (*the capital city of the Northern Song Dynasty*)	wǔ shù 武術	martial arts
		mǎ tóu 碼頭	dock; pier
xiàng 巷	lane; alley	xiè huò 卸貨	unload or discharge cargo
yíng yè 營業	do business	suàn mìng 算命	fortune-telling
sì 肆	*another name for shop in the Northern Song Dynasty*	xián liáo 閑聊	chat
		gōng tíng 宮廷	imperial court
yú lè 娛樂	entertainment	nán dé 難得	rare

Lesson 12

Five Dynasties and Ten Kingdoms and the Northern Song Dynasty

When the Tang Dynasty ended, China split into many small states. During more than five decades after Tang, five larger states controlled the areas along the Yellow River in succession, and are known as "Five Dynasties" of Later Liang, Later Tang, Later Jin, Later Han, and Later Zhou. At the same time, nine kingdoms were founded in South China including Wu, Southern Tang and Chu, together with Northern Han in Shanxi, are known in history as the "Ten Kingdoms."

In A.D. 960, Zhao Kuangyin seized power from the emperor of Later Zhou and founded the Song Dynasty, which is now known in history as the Northern Song Dynasty, with the capital city of Kaifeng. In A.D. 979, the Northern Song Dynasty unified the entire country and ended the Five Dynasties and Ten Kingdoms, a period of time when countries and states were split from one another.

After founding the Northern Song Dynasty, Zhao Kuangyin, the first emperor of the Song Dynasty, had learned a lesson from the Five Dynasties and the Ten Kingdoms where warlords caused the splitting of the entire country, and he did not want to see an emperor's position being threatened by military generals again. He then disarmed all his generals at a banquet and ruled the army directly. He also constructed a complete civil official system for the country's administration process, and started the tradition of emphasizing administrative merits instead of military achievements. The imperial examination system during the Song Dynasty was relatively strict. With this system, many low-born people who were gifted were selected to be officials, and those without genuine ability and talent found it difficult to pass. This system helped the government to find many talents, but also contributed to the formation of a social value system where "no life deserved praise, and only scholars are of noble caliber."

In the middle of the Northern Song Dynasty, the degree of land concentration was extremely high and half of the farmers didn't even have their own land, resulting in discontentment which led to many uprisings. Due to its failures in the wars against Liao and Xia, the Song government had to cede some of its territory and offer annual tributes to both Liao and Xia. To make things worse, it required a lot of money to support both the military force and the numerous government officials, which caused the government to suffer financial difficulties. Because of the serious political and social situation in the country, reformist Wang Anshi started to implement reforms in A.D. 1069 with the emperor's support. The reforms focused mainly on financial and military management. As part of their financial reforms, the state offered low-interest loan to farmers, constructed water conservancy projects, and re-measured the area of land to make taxation more reasonable. The state also implemented some military reforms by reducing the amount of soldiers in the army and improved military combat power. However, these reform measures promoted by Wang Anshi ended in failure due to severe objection of the conservatives.

During the late Northern Song Dynasty, Emperor Huizong was known for his painting and calligraphy. He was extremely talented in art, and he loved flowers, stones, bamboo, and woods. Because of this, he ordered the construction of large scale gardens in the capital city. However, he was hopeless in ruling a country and gullibly trusted treacherous people, which resulted in a politically dark period towards the end of the Northern Song Dynasty.

Meanwhile, the Nuzhen nationality founded the Jin Kingdom in the north, which grew rapidly and eventually destroyed the Kingdom of Liao in A.D. 1125. During the same year after defeating Liao, Jin sent an army to fight against Song. Emperor Huizong had no other option but to fight back. He abdicated the throne to his crown prince (later known as Emperor Qinzong). Under the leadership of General Li Gang, the Northern Song army finally defeated Jin. But the incompetent Emperor Huizong and Qinzong wanted to make peace with Jin so they dismissed Li Gang and promised to cede territory and pay indemnities and Jin retreated. But in A.D. 1127, Jin once again marched toward the south, took over Kaifeng and seized both Emperor Huizong and Qinzong together with over 3,000 other people including empresses, imperial concubines, ministers, officials, and a large amount of valuables. The Northern Song Dynasty thus came to an end.

Although continuous wars plagued North China during the Northern Song Dynasty, South China enjoyed peace and there was obvious progress in the field of science and technology. For example, one of the Four Great Inventions known as the moveable-type printing technique was invented during this period, and gunpowder was invented for military use for the first time due to the needs of war. The literary and artistic achievements during this period are also significant. The Song Ci poetry enjoyed the same great fame with poetry produced during the Tang Dynasty and is regarded as precious Chinese classical literary treasure. As for the field of painting and calligraphy, Zhang Zeduan's *Chinese Symphonic Picture Riverside Scene at Qingming Festival* depict scenes of Bianjing (Kaifeng) during the festival with nearly 600 figures in the picture, making it a great work in the history of Chinese painting.

Flourishing Cities

Although the north fought with Liao frequently during the Northern Song Dynasty, people in the central plains and in the south could still live peaceful and affluent lives. Commerce during the Song Dynasty developed significantly and it was a business giant in the world at that time.

During the Song Dynasty, cities of differing scale were sprouting up everywhere in ports and around main traffic hubs due to the growth and development of the handicraft industry and other businesses, creating a large business exchange network. For example, some cities and towns were famous for paper products and shoes, while others enjoyed a developed printing industry, and a few others were famous for making bamboo baskets and matting. The exchange of commodities among these cities and towns promoted the development of a traffic system. At that time, there were a large amount of floating population which led to a rise in numerous hotels, restaurants, tea houses, and shops, creating flourishing and lively cities and towns.

The capital city of Bianjing during the Northern Song Dynasty was a famous big city in the world at that time, with a total of 200,000 households and numerous shops, hotels, and restaurants that open late into the night. There were also entertainment places named "Wa Si" where people could enjoy traditional opera, acrobatics, and martial arts performances. The city remained lively during night and morning markets started even before the sun rose. The city was indeed hustling and bustling with business activity. The famous painting *Chinese Symphonic Picture Riverside Scene at Qingming Festival* vividly captured the city life of the Song Dynasty.

Chinese Symphonic Picture Riverside Scene at Qingming Festival

The *Chinese Symphonic Picture Riverside Scene at Qingming Festival* by Zhang Zeduan, a famous painter during the Song Dynasty, is a very famous painting in the history of China. Zhang Zeduan lived during the Northern Song Dynasty and used to live in the capital city of Bianjing when he was younger. He learned to paint and favored especially themes of houses, cities, vehicles, boats, rivers, and roads.

When the Northern Song Dynasty ended, many fled to the south, and Zhang Zeduan was one of them. Whenever he recalled the natural views and people along the Bianhe River during the Qingming Festival in Bianjing, he would miss his hometown very much and painted all he remembered of Bianjing from memory. The scroll is 5.25m long and 0.255m high.

The picture is well painted and reproduces the true way of life in Bianjing. The picture shows that there are farming areas, roads, bridges across the river, and boats of different sizes transporting grains and commodities along both banks of the Bianhe River. Workers on docks are busy loading and unloading cargos, and camels and horse-drawn carriages come and go busy doing business. Shops and stores selling grains, meat, and fruits are everywhere and there is even a fortune-teller among the crowd... the painter had indeed drawn the business district along the Bianhe River as a place bustling with different kinds of activities.

If one looks further into the painting, one will be able to notice more details like a wedding team with a bridal sedan chair in the center, or a group of people gathering around a stage for performance, adults and kids enjoying a monk's martial art performance, and people drinking tea and chatting with friends at a tea house. Behind the imperial palace wall, the empress is seen to be boarding the dragon boat touring the lake with the help of court maids… Indeed every single detail is vividly depicted.

When you look at the scroll, it seems that you're actually walking along the Bianhe River and seeing with your own eyes a flourishing street, as well as the lives of ordinary people and the imperial family of the Song Dynasty. It is really a precious scroll painting with both intrinsic historical and artistic value.

第十三課

遼、西夏、金與南宋

宋朝當時的主要敵人有三個：遼國、西夏、金國。

遼是契丹人建立的。契丹族是中國古代北方的少數民族，原住在遼河一帶，以遊牧和漁獵為生。唐末，許多中原漢人因躲避戰亂而遷移到契丹境内。他們帶去了先進的生產技術和漢族文化，使契丹人學會了種田、紡織、冶鐵、建房屋，開始了農耕和定居的生活。除此之外，契丹人深受漢文化影響，創造了文字，建立孔廟並尊儒學。公元907年，契丹八部落統一。公元916年契丹人建立國家機構並立年號，後把國名改為遼。遼國很快強大起來。公元1004年，遼軍20萬南下攻宋，宋真宗親自出征，結果雙方議和，規定：宋每年給遼白銀10萬兩，絹20萬匹；邊境維持現狀。公元1125年，遼國被金國消滅。

《出行圖》局部
（遼墓壁畫）

西夏是由西北地區一個少數民族黨項族建立的。五代時，黨

項族首領李元昊(hào)建立夏（史稱西夏）。李元昊注意學習先進的漢文化和宋朝的制度，並命人創造了西夏文字。西夏、宋之間經常發生戰爭，後雙方議和，西夏對宋稱臣，宋朝每年給西夏白銀7.2萬兩，絹15.3萬匹，茶3萬斤。從此西夏和宋朝之間和平了。公元1227年，西夏被蒙古消滅。

金國是女真族建立的。女真族居住在長白山和黑龍江一帶，受遼的控制。女真人不甘心受遼的壓迫，起兵反遼，於公元1115年建立金國。十年後，金國軍隊消滅了遼國，佔領了遼的土地。

在消滅遼國後，金看到了北宋的腐敗無能，開始進攻宋。公元1126年年底，金軍攻佔宋的都城汴京，宋欽宗投降。公元1127年，金軍俘虜了宋朝皇帝徽宗、欽宗父子，北宋滅亡。

妙音鳥（西夏王陵出土）

宋徽宗的另一個兒子於公元1127年在臨安（今杭州）繼承皇位，建立南宋，他就是宋高

宗。南宋朝廷害怕金兵，只想偏安求和，不想返回中原了。可是中原的人民紛紛拿起武器組成抗金義軍。著名將領韓世忠、岳飛等多次打敗金軍。特別是岳飛領導的“岳家軍”，勇猛善戰，收復了大片失地。正當抗金鬥爭順利發展的時候，宋高宗和宰相秦檜(huì)，害怕抗金力量壯大起來會威脅自己的統治，於是，一邊下命令停止北伐，召回岳飛，一邊向金求和。岳飛一回到臨安就被宋高宗解除了兵權。秦檜還以謀反罪將岳飛殺害。岳飛英勇抗金的一生，得到了廣大人民的尊敬。

金和南宋長期戰爭，雙方都被削弱。這使北方的蒙古族有機會發展壯大起來。蒙古騎兵與金軍交戰，節節勝利。公元1234年，蒙古軍隊消滅了金國。

《岳飛抗金》 王金泰 畫

成吉思汗的

孫子忽必烈於公元1271年建立元朝。接著，元軍向南宋發動進攻並佔領了都城臨安，統一了全中國。但是南宋的大臣文天祥等人繼續抵抗。後來，文天祥被元軍捉住，他視死如歸，寫下了千古流芳的詩句“人生自古誰無死，留取丹心照汗青”，然後從容就義。

公元1279年，宋軍在廣東最後戰敗，南宋滅亡。

兩宋技術和文化的發展

宋朝長期受遼、西夏和金的侵略，軍力不及強鄰，但是經濟文化發達，水平遠在這些民族之上。

兩宋時期雖然戰爭不斷，但是生產還是有所發展，科學技術也有明顯的進步。例如宋朝的陶瓷業和造船業都很先進，宋還有當時世界第一的採礦業和冶鐵業。發明於唐代的火藥到宋朝時已廣泛應用，比歐洲使用火藥早了300年。

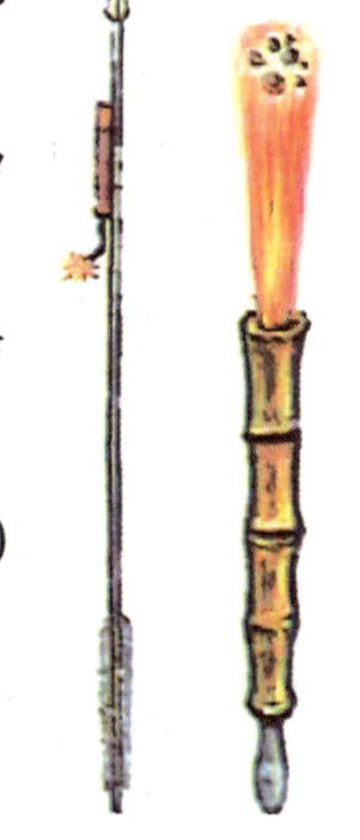
火箭與突火槍

官窑琮式瓶

宋代，生產工具有了改進，又推廣種植占城稻，增加了水稻產量。當時茶成為主

交子（宋）

要的經濟作物，製茶業也相當發達，茶葉成為與少數民族交易的主要商品。另外，紡織、造紙、印刷等行業都有顯著發展，特别是畢昇發明了活字印刷術，大大提高了印刷速度。北宋還出現了世界上最早的紙幣——交子，比歐洲發行的鈔票早600多年。

生詞

拼音	生詞	English
qì dān	契丹	Qidan (*nationality*)
wéi chí	維持	maintain
dǎng xiàng	黨項	Dangxiang (*nationality*)
fú lǔ	俘虜	take captive; capture
běi fá	北伐	northern expedition
zhào huí	召回	recall
wén tiān xiáng	文天祥	Wen Tianxiang (*name*)
qiān gǔ liú fāng	千古流芳	leave a good name to posterity
cóng róng	從容	calm
jiù yì	就義	die a hero's death
qīn lüè	侵略	invade
yìng yòng	應用	apply; put to use
tuī guǎng	推廣	extend; popularize
fā xíng	發行	issue; distribute
chāo piào	鈔票	banknote

聽寫

邊境　維持　黨項族　鈔票　從容　應用　召回

千古流芳　北伐　*俘虜　推廣

比一比

境 { 邊境 / 環境 }　　維 { 維持 / 維生素 }　　{ 鈔（鈔票） / 吵（争吵） }　　{ 祥（文天祥） / 詳（詳細） }

容 { 從容 / 容易 }　　略 { 侵略 / 謀略 }　　{ 召（召回） / 招（招呼） }　　{ 芳（千古流芳） / 方（方向） }

詞語運用

順利

小芳順利地通過了考試。

應用

計算機技術得到普遍的應用。

多音字

yìng 應	yīng 應
yìng 應用	yīng 應該

回答問題

1. 遼、西夏和金分別是什麼民族建立的國家?

2. 岳飛是南宋最著名的抗金將領，請説一説關於他的故事。

3. 文天祥被金軍捉住後，他怎樣面對死亡?

4. 請舉例説一説兩宋科技、文化發展的情況。

詞語解釋

邊境——靠近邊界的地方。

壓迫——用權力或勢力強制別人服從。

謀反——暗中謀劃反叛。

視死如歸——把死看作回家一樣。形容不怕死。

閱讀

民族英雄岳飛

岳飛（1103—1142），河南湯陰人，少年的時候勤奮好學，練出了一身好武藝，在抗金戰鬥中立下很多戰功，升為元帥。人們把岳飛的軍隊叫做“岳家軍”。“岳家軍”作戰勇敢，收復了鄭州、洛陽等地。金軍對他們十分害怕。

岳飛像

岳飛一生，親自指揮打了126仗，從來没有失敗過，是名副其實的常勝將軍。一次，岳飛與金軍鐵騎兵作戰，大破敵軍。金軍士兵感嘆道：“撼山易，撼岳家軍難。”

正當岳飛招兵買馬，積極準備渡過黄河，打敗金軍，收復失地的時候，宋高宗連發十二道金牌，命令岳飛退兵。岳飛無可奈何，只好揮淚班師。岳飛回到臨安以後，馬上就被解除了兵權。高宗和秦檜派人向金求和，金兀术要求“必先殺岳飛，方可議和”。秦檜誣陷岳飛謀反，將岳飛關進監獄毒死，那年岳飛僅僅三十九歲。他的兒子岳雲也同時被害。

岳飛一生文武雙全，品德高尚，熱愛祖國，千百年來被人們稱做英雄；而殺害他的奸臣秦檜，則世代被人唾罵。

生詞

qín fèn	勤奮	diligent	bān shī	班師	withdraw troops from the front line
zhǐ huī	指揮	command	jīn wù zhú	金兀术	Jin Wuzhu (*name*)
míng fù qí shí	名副其實	live up to one's reputation	qín huì	秦檜	Qin Hui (*name*)
hàn	撼	shake	wū xiàn	誣陷	frame; incriminate an innocent person
jīn pái	金牌	gold plaque (*issued to generals as imperial authorization for troop movement in ancient China*); gold medal	tuò mà	唾罵	spit on and curse

English Translation

Lesson 13

Liao, West Xia, Jin, and the Southern Song Dynasty

The Song government had to deal with three main enemies: the Kingdom of Liao, the West Xia, and the Kingdom of Jin.

Liao was founded by the Qidan people, a minority living in the north of ancient China. They used to live around the Liaohe River, and were nomads that survived on fishing and hunting. During the late Tang Dynasty, many of Han nationality who lived in the central plains moved to the territory claimed by Qidan in order to avoid war. They brought along with them the advanced production technologies and culture of Han nationality. Since then, the Qidan people learned farming, weaving, smelting, and building houses, and settled down there. In addition, with the profound impact of the Han culture, the Qidan people invented a written language, and constructed temples dedicated to Confucius. In A.D. 907, the eight tribes of the Qidan nationality were unified. The Qidan people founded their own kingdom in A.D. 916 and changed their name to Liao. The Kingdom of Liao grew rapidly and in A.D. 1004, it sent a 200,000 strong army to the south to attack Song, forcing Emperor Zhenzong himself onto the battlefield. Later on, they made peace with each other on the condition that the Song government offered Liao 100,000 *liang* of silver and 200,000 *pi* of thin silk each year. The border resumed peace and in A.D. 1125, Liao was destroyed by the Kingdom of Jin.

The West Xia was founded by the Dangxiang nationality, a minority in the northwestern area of China. During the period of the Five Dynasties, Li Yuanhao, the chief of the Dangxiang nationality at that time, founded Xia (known in history as West Xia). Li Yuanhao learned the advanced culture of the Han nationality and systems of the Song Dynasty, and ordered the invention of a written language for West Xia. West Xia fought with Song frequently but they finally made peace with each other. West Xia submitted to Song on the condition that the Song government offered them 72,000 *liang* of silver, 153,000 *pi* of thin silk, and 30,000 *jin* of tea each year. Peace maintained between West Xia and Song until West Xia was destroyed by Mongolia in A.D. 1227.

The Kingdom of Jin was founded by the Nuzhen nationality living in the area of Changbai Mountain and Heilongjiang River. It was once controlled by Liao. Reluctant to be oppressed by Liao, they rose up against Liao and founded the Kingdom of Jin in A.D. 1115. Ten years later, the army of Jin destroyed Liao and took over all of its territory.

After destroying Liao and witnessing the corruption and incompetence of the Northern Song government, Jin launched an attack on Song. At the end of A.D. 1126, Jin seized the capital city Bianjing, and Emperor Qinzong of the Song Dynasty surrendered. In A.D. 1127, Jin captured Emperor Huizong and Qinzong and the Northern Song Dynasty came to an end.

Another son of Emperor Huizong came to the throne in A.D. 1127 in Lin'an (today's Hangzhou) and founded the Southern Song Dynasty and he became known as Emperor Gaozong of the Song Dynasty. The Southern Song government was afraid of Jin and was eager to make peace instead of fighting all the way back to the central plains. But people in the central plains rose up to take arms and organized an army against Jin. Well-known generals, Han Shizhong and Yue Fei, defeated the army of Jin many times. The Army of the Yue Family led by Yue Fei was especially good at fighting and recovered a lot of lost territory. Emperor Gaozong and Prime Minister Qin Hui saw this and started to fear that the increasingly powerful force against Jin would threaten their rule. They ordered the expedition to the north to stop and called Yue Fei back to court. Meanwhile, they engaged in a negotiation with Jin. Upon his return to Lin'an, Yue Fei was disarmed by Emperor Gao Zong and was killed by Qin Hui under the false charge of conspiring against imperial rule. Yue Fei nevertheless gained respect among ordinary people for dedicating his life to fighting against Jin.

After engaging in many wars over a long period of time, both the kingdom of Jin and the Southern Song Dynasty declined, giving the Mongolian nationality in the north an opportunity to grow rapidly. The Mongolian cavalry fought with Jin and in A.D. 1234, Mongolia destroyed the kingdom of Jin.

Kublai Khan, the grandson of Genghis Khan, founded the Yuan Dynasty in A.D. 1271 and attacked Southern Song and captured the capital city of Lin'an, unifiying the entire country. However, Minister Wen Tianxiang and other people of the Southern Song Dynasty fought back continuously until Wen Tianxiang was captured by the Yuan empire. He faced death unflinchingly and wrote a well-known poem which ended with two famous lines: "Everyone will die in the end, but I'll leave a loyal heart that shines in the pages of history." He died in the exact way he advocated in the poem.

In A.D. 1279, the army of Song lost the final battle in Guangdong and the Southern Song Dynasty came to the end.

Technological and Cultural Development during two Song Dynasties

Song was invaded by Liao, West Xia, and Jin for a long period of time and suffered inferior military power but its economy and culture were more developed and superior than these minorities.

During the two Song Dynasties, the country suffered continuous wars but still managed to develop in production, and progress in the field of science and technology. For example, both the ceramic industry and the ship-building industry during the Song Dynasty were highly developed. Its mining and smelting industry ranked first in the world at that time. Gunpowder invented during the Tang Dynasty was extensively applied during the Song Dynasty, 300 years earlier than Europe.

During the Song Dynasty, production tools were greatly improved. The output of rice increased greatly due to the extensive promotion of Zhancheng rice. Tea became one of the leading economic crops at the time and the tea industry was extremely developed, making tea leaves the main commodity that was traded with other smaller products. In addition to this, the textile, paper-making, and printing industries also showed considerable progress, and especially after the invention of moveable-type printing technique by Bi Sheng, the printing speed rose greatly. The Northern Song Dynasty also produced the first paper money in the world which was known as *jiao-zi*, which was 600 years earlier than the first bill issued in Europe.

Yue Fei, a National Hero

Yue Fei (1103-1142) was born in Tangyin, Henan. He was diligent and eager to learn when he was young, and was especially good at martial arts. He was promoted to the position of supreme commander due to his numerous merits in battles against Jin. People called his men "The Army of the Yue Family." He led his valiant army to recover Zhengzhou and Luoyang and Jin was extremely afraid of them.

During his lifetime, Yue Fei commanded a total of 126 battles and was never defeated by his enemies even once, and this won him the fame of "The Ever-Victorious General." One day, Yue Fei led his men to fighting the cavalry of Jin and defeated them. His enemy sighed and said, "To move a mountain is much easier than to defeat 'The Army of the Yue Family'."

When Yue Fei was recruiting more men as his soldiers and buying horses in preparation of the crossing of the Yellow River to defeat Jin and recover lost territory, he was ordered to return 12 times in the form of 12 gold plaques by Emperor Gaozong. Yue Fei could do nothing else but retreat. Upon returning to Lin'an, Yue Fei was immediately disarmed. Meanwhile, Emperor Gaozong and Qin Hui sent a messenger to make peace with Jin, while Jin Wuzhu insisted on "killing Yue Fei before any negotiation could be made." Qin Hui then maliciously prosecuted Yue Fei for conspiring against imperial rule and threw him in prison before poisoning him. Yue Fei was only 39 when he died, and his son Yue Yun was also killed.

Yue Fei was good at both letters and martial arts. He was noble and loved his home country. He has been respected as a hero for more than 1,000 years, while Qin Hui, the treacherous court official who persecuted him, was spit upon and cursed for generations.

第十四課

成吉思汗和他的子孫

蒙古族本來是一個生活在蒙古草原上的遊牧民族。12世紀時，蒙古的各個部落之間戰爭不斷，其中一個部落打敗了其他部落，成為最強大的部落，這個部落的首領叫鐵木真。公元1206年，蒙古部落首領大會推舉鐵木真為成吉思汗①，從此蒙古建立了統一的政權，創造了蒙古文字。

成吉思汗像

蒙古的強大是有原因的。蒙古人生活在土地貧瘠（jí），氣候嚴寒的漠北②。他們依靠騎射的本領奔馳在草原上，練成了吃苦、尚武的精神。同時，蒙古成長壯大的時候，四周沒有強國。鄰近的宋、金、西夏之間常年打仗，互相削弱；西亞各國處在長期混亂之中；東羅馬帝國衰落以後，歐洲沒有統一的國家。這一切給了成吉思汗一個絕好的機會。公元1219年，成吉思

---

① 成吉思汗——成吉思，蒙語，意思是“強大”；“汗”是可汗的簡稱。

② 漠北——古代指蒙古高原大沙漠以北地區。

汗率領蒙古軍隊進行了第一次西征，佔領了今俄羅斯至伊朗西北境的廣大地區。他又帶領蒙古騎兵於公元1227年消滅了西夏。在蒙古軍隊就要攻克西夏的時候，65歲的成吉思汗病死。

蒙古騎兵

成吉思汗死後，他的第三個兒子窩闊臺繼承了汗位。公元1234年蒙古又滅了金國。公元1235年至1244年，蒙古軍隊又進行了一次西征。成吉思汗的一個孫子拔都，率兵征服了今俄羅斯、匈牙利等地，一直打到柏林附近和亞得里亞海濱，震動了整個歐洲。成吉思汗的另一個孫子旭烈兀於公元1253年至1259年第三次西征。他攻佔了巴格達等地，建立了伊兒汗國[①]。成吉思汗的子孫們又繼續南征，打敗了南宋等許多國家，建立了地跨歐亞的蒙古大帝國，國土面積有3,000多萬平方公里。蒙古帝國東起白令海峽，西到萊茵河，北到北冰洋，南到波斯灣。其

窩闊臺即位圖

① 伊兒汗國——有的史書也稱為“伊利汗國”。

領土除了今天的中國和蒙古外，還包括了朝鮮半島、俄羅斯、東歐、伊朗、伊拉克、土耳其、緬甸、巴基斯坦等國家。但是，到成吉思汗的孫子輩時，蒙古帝國實際上已分為元帝國和四大汗國。

公元1260年，成吉思汗的孫子忽必烈繼位，史稱元世祖。公元1271年，改國號為“大元”並遷都大都（dū）（今北京），從此，北京漸漸成為中國政治、經濟和文化的中心。

生詞

yóu mù 遊牧	nomadic	běi bīng yáng 北冰洋	the Arctic Ocean
bēn chí 奔馳	run quickly	yī lǎng 伊朗	Iran (*country*)
hùn luàn 混亂	chaos	yī lā kè 伊拉克	Iraq (*country*)
xiōng yá lì 匈牙利	Hungary (*country*)	tǔ ěr qí 土耳其	Turkey (*country*)
xù liè wù 旭烈兀	Hulagu (*name*)	miǎn diàn 緬甸	Myanmar (*country*)
kuà 跨	cut across; go beyond	bā jī sī tǎn 巴基斯坦	Pakistan (*country*)
lái yīn hé 萊茵河	Rhine River		

聽寫

奔馳　匈牙利　跨　北冰洋　伊朗　伊拉克　緬甸　混亂

巴基斯坦　征服　*旭烈兀　萊茵河

比一比

征｛征服　征兵　出征｝

聯｛聯盟　聯合　聯繫｝

洋｛北冰洋　太平洋　得意洋洋｝

｛遊（遊牧）　游（游泳）｝

基｛巴基斯坦　基礎｝

伊｛伊拉克　伊朗｝

｛跨（跨越）　誇（誇獎）｝

｛匈（匈牙利）　胸（胸有成竹）｝

詞語運用

本領

他射擊的本領高強，百發百中。

跨

他飛快地跨越一個個欄架，衝向終點，取得了冠軍。

世界上很多大公司都是跨國公司。

回答問題

1. 元朝的首都是現在的哪個城市?

2. 為什麼蒙古能強大起來? 請說一説其中的原因。

詞語解釋

本領——技能；能力。

吃苦——經受艱苦。

尚武——注重軍事或武術。

絶好——極好；最好。

閱讀

中西交通

中國對外交通，開始於漢代的絲綢之路。到了隋唐，對外交通除了陸路還有海路。宋代陸路交通中斷，但海路貿易繁榮。元代蒙古人征服了很多的民族，國土空前遼闊，各民族之間語言不通，但是在當時，如果一個人通曉蒙古語，可由歐洲到達中國，一路之上交流毫無阻礙。自此，“世界”大通，東西文化互相影響。中國的發明西傳，西方近代文化開始東來。

元政府在交通大道上修建驛站。每隔幾十里設一個驛站，給宣佈政令的人員和來往的商人們提供食宿和餵馬的草料。東西大道長一萬多里，沿途都有驛站，所以政令的發布和商旅的往來都很方便、暢通。據説，還有一條通過雲南去阿拉伯半島的陸路。至於海道，自元世祖允許國際商貿往來以後，商船從中國沿海出發經印度洋可以到達波斯灣。中國在廣州、杭州、温州、泉州設立了七個市舶司，管理中外貿易。大都成為國際性都市，泉州成為當時世界上最大的海港。海運業一時特别發達。

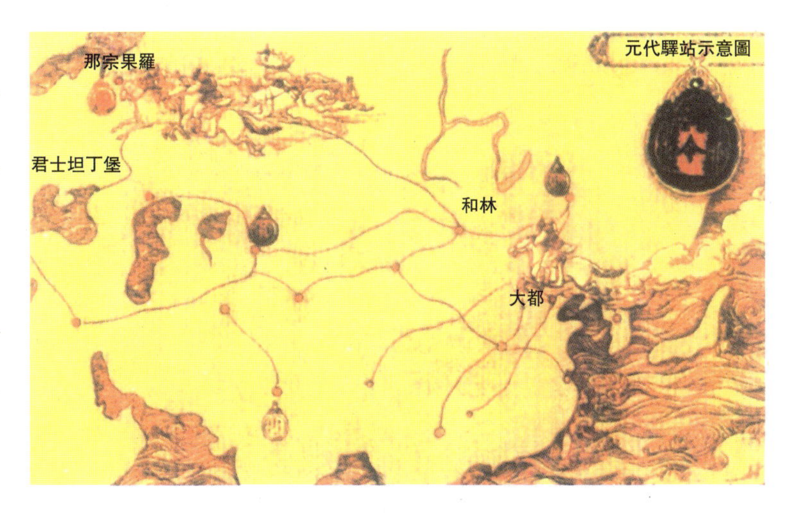

生詞

tōngxiǎo 通曉	thoroughly understand	chàng tōng 暢通	unblocked; unimpeded
zǔ ài 阻礙	hinder; obstacle	bàn dǎo 半島	peninsula
xuān bù 宣佈	declare; announce	shì bó sī 市舶司	Maritime Trade Supervisory Department
tí gōng 提供	provide; supply	yì shí 一時	a period of time

Lesson 14

Genghis Khan and His Descendants

The Mongolian nationality used to be a nomadic community that lived on Mongolian grassland. In the 12th Century, war broke out among different Mongolian tribes. Finally, one dominant tribe defeated all the others and became the most powerful tribe amongst them. The chieftain of the tribe was Temujin. In A.D. 1206, a conference was held between the Mongolian chieftains, and Temujin was elected to be Genghis Khan. Since then, Mongolia became a unified country with a newly invented written language.

There were reasons behind the rising of Mongolia. Mongolians lived in the north desert area where the land was barren and climate was cold and frigid. They lived on the grassland areas, depending on their riding skill and archery for survival and this fostered the tough character and warrior spirit within them. Another reason that contributed to their rapid growth was due to the fact that there was no powerful force around that might serve as a threat. Its neighbors — Song, Jin, and West Xia fought with each other continuously and declined significantly after many years of war. Countries in West Asia also suffered much internal disorder for a long period of time. After the decline of the Eastern Roman empire, there was no other unified country in Europe. All these factors provided a good opportunity for Genghis Khan to develop the Mongolian nation. In A.D. 1219, Genghis Khan led his Mongolian army on its first expedition to the west and took over a vast area of today's Russia to the northwest border of Iran. He then led his Mongolian cavalry to destroy West Xia in A.D. 1227. However, just as his army was about to seize West Xia, Genghis Khan died of illness at the age of 65.

After the death of Genghis Khan, his third son Ogodei Khan succeeded to the throne. In A.D. 1234, Mongolia destroyed the Kingdom of Jin. The Mongolian army launched another expedition to the west during A.D. 1235 to A.D. 1244. Batu Khan, one of Genghis Khan's grandson, led the army and conquered today's Russia and Hungary, marching close to Berlin and the Adriatic Coast, shaking the entire Europe. Hulagu Khan, another grandson of Genghis Khan, led the third expedition to the west during A.D. 1253 to A.D. 1259. He took over Baghdad and founded the Kingdom of Il-Khan. The descendants of Genghis Khan explored the south continuously and took over many countries there, including the Southern Song Dynasty, and founded the great Mongolian Empire spanning both Europe and Asia with a total territory of more than 30 million square kilometers. The Mongolian empire covered over an extensive area that bordered the Bering Strait in the east, the Rhine River in the west, the Arctic Ocean in the north, and the Persian Gulf in the south. Apart from today's China and Mongolia, its territory also included the Korean Peninsular, Russia, East Europe, Iran, Iraq, Turkey, Burma, and Pakistan. In the hands of the grandsons of Genghis Khan, the Mongolian empire was, however, actually divided into the Yuan Empire and the four Kingdoms of Khan.

In A.D. 1260, Kublai Khan, the grandson of Genghis Khan, succeeded the throne and was later known as Emperor Shizu of the Yuan Dynasty. In A.D. 1271, the Dynasty was renamed as "Da Yuan" and moved its capital city to Dadu (today's Beijing). Since then, Beijing became the political, economic, and cultural center of China.

Communications between China and the West

Communication between China and other countries started first from the construction of the Silk Road during the Han Dynasty. Apart from the land transportation and communication routes, the seaborne communication route was also developed during the Sui and Tang Dynasties. During the Song Dynasty, the land route was stopped but the marine trade flourished. During the Yuan Dynasty, the Mongolian army conquered numerous nationalities and enjoyed unprecedented vast territory. Different nationalities spoke their own languages. But if a man was proficient in Mongolian at that time, he could travel from China to Europe without any obstacle in communication. This made the world smaller as the western and eastern cultures were close as they interacted actively with each other. Chinese inventions were passed to the west and the modern western culture likewise influenced the eastern world.

The Yuan government built post-houses along the main roads and every dozen of *li* there will be one post-house that could provide accommodation for businessmen or people delivering government orders, as well as a stopover to feed their horses. The main east-west road at the time was about 10,000 *li* long with post-houses along the road, making it convenient and smooth for the distribution of government orders, and for traveling businessmen. It is also said that there was another land route at that time that could reach Arabia through Yunnan. There was also significant growth in the maritime trade industry at that time. Since Emperor Shizu of the Yuan Dynasty allowed international business exchanges, merchant ships could start from the coastal area of China and reach Persian Gulf by crossing the Indian Ocean. China established seven Maritime Trade Supervisory Departments in Guangzhou, Hangzhou, Wenzhou, and Quanzhou in order to regulate foreign trade. Dadu became an international metropolitan center and Quanzhou was the biggest seaport in the world. The maritime industry indeed flourished greatly at that time.

第十五課

元

忽必烈建立的元朝是蒙古族的王朝，也是中國歷史上第一個少數民族統治全國的政權。在中國歷史上，元朝的疆土比以往任何朝代都要遼闊。忽必烈是一位傑出的皇帝，他清楚地看到，在成吉思汗赫赫武功的背後，是蒙古人治理國家經驗的不足和觀念的落後。於是他重用漢人，大力推行漢法，使元朝面貌一新。

忽必烈像

為了管理這個遼闊的國家，元朝建立了行(xíng)省制度：中央設中書省管理全國政務；地方設行省，皇帝派官員管理。行省制度使邊遠地區和內地一

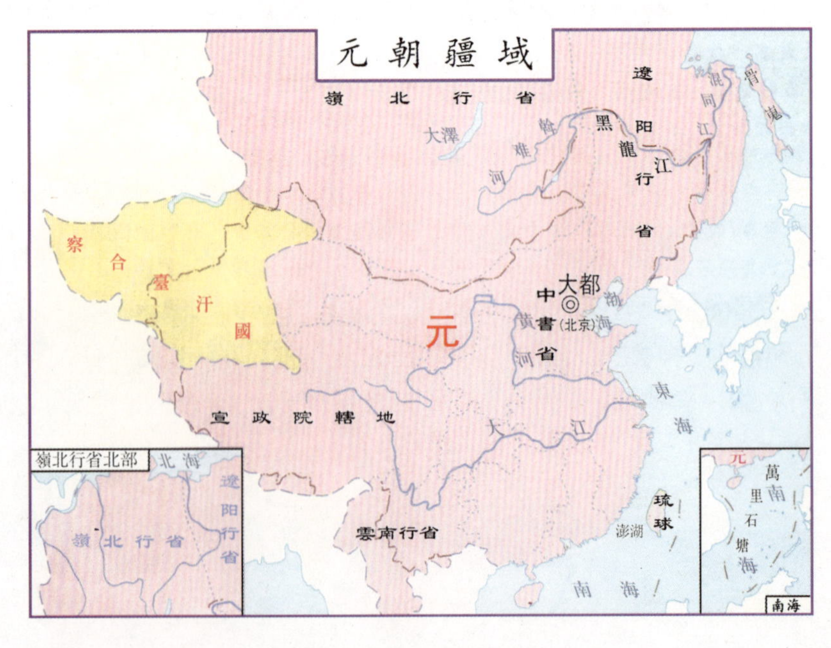

樣，受到國家的管理並向國家交納賦稅。

元朝時，今天的西藏成為元的正式行政區。那裏有元朝官員清查户口和收税。公元1360年，元朝設立了澎湖巡檢司，管理澎湖列島和琉球（今台灣）。

忽必烈還實行勸農的政策，使農業得到恢復和發展。蒙古族本是一個遊牧民族，進入黄河流域農業區以後，他們把漢人趕走，讓田地長出綠草，好放牧牛羊。但是忽必烈卻下令保護農業，把牧場退還為農田；還成立了"勸農司"，專門鼓勵老百姓開墾田地，種桑養蠶，從而使農業生產不斷恢復和發展。

忽必烈提倡以儒學為主的漢族傳統文化。他年輕時就受到儒家文化的影響，常請儒士來講解儒學的道理。繼位以後，他下令建立孔廟，恢復學校，還設立國子學，用漢族文化教育蒙古官員的子弟。正是由於忽必烈大力推行漢法，纔使草原上建立起來的大蒙古國終於轉變成了元王朝。

馬可·波羅告别元世祖回國

中統元寶交鈔——元代紙幣

元朝中期，海外貿易空前發達。由於東西方來往的道路通行無阻，歐亞之間的商業活動相當活躍。中國的印刷術、火藥等傳到西方，西方文化也隨著商人傳到中國。那時的北京，有許多外國商人和使節長期居住。元代，意大利人馬可·波羅寫了一本《馬可·波羅遊記》，轟動了歐洲。在這本書中，他介紹了在中國17年的經歷和見聞，使歐洲人開始認識中國。此外，海運、漕運和商業的繁榮，以及紙幣的流行，使元朝成為當時世界上最富庶的國家之一。

元代的科學技術和文學藝術也都有發展。天文學家郭守敬制訂的《授時曆》推算出一年有365.2425日，與現行的公曆相同。元朝，在中國南方，棉花種植已經非常普遍，出現了一大批棉紡織手工業者，其中最著名的是黄道婆。黄道婆推廣、改進了紡車、織機和棉紡織技術，棉布在中國得以大量生產。元代文化最著名的是元曲，它是中國現代戲曲的開端，代表作品有關漢卿(qīng)的《竇娥(é)冤》、王實甫(fǔ)的《西廂記》等。

銅火銃(chòng)

不過，元朝為了保住蒙古貴族的地位，實行了民族歧視和壓

迫的政策。元朝把全國人民分為四個等級，最高等的是蒙古人，其次為色目人，第三等為漢人，最低等的是南人[1]。漢人和南人在政治上、法律上或科舉考試方面都受到歧視。這個政策很不得人心，也加深了民族矛盾。忽必烈死後，其後代爭奪帝位的鬥爭激烈，加上連年災荒，終於爆發了紅巾軍起義。義軍領袖朱元璋(zhāng)於公元1368年在今南京稱帝，建立明朝。同年，起義軍攻入元大都，元朝滅亡。

明代刻本《西厢記》插圖

---

① 元朝的“色目人”指中亞、西亞、歐洲以及當時吐蕃(bō)等許多民族，“漢人”主要指原金朝統治下的漢族、契丹、女真等民族，“南人”主要指原南宋統治下的人民。

生詞

hè hè wǔ gōng 赫赫武功	impressive military achievements	cáo yùn 漕運	water transport of grain to the capital (*in feudal times*)
miàn mào 面貌	appearance	zhì dìng 制訂	formulate
jiǎn chá 檢（查）	examine; check	xì qǔ 戲曲	traditional opera
péng hú liè dǎo 澎湖列島	Penghu Islands	dòu 竇	Dou (*surname*)
kāi kěn 開墾	open up or reclaim (*wasteland*)	xiāng 廂	wing-room; compartment
sāng 桑	mulberry	qí shì 歧視	discrimination
tí chàng 提倡	advocate	lǐng xiù 領袖	leader
huó yuè 活躍	vibrant		
jīng lì 經歷	experience		

聽寫

活躍　提倡　經歷　檢（查）　等級　（車）廂　以往

見聞　激烈　領袖　*開墾　澎湖

比一比

倡（提倡）	墾（開墾）	檢（檢查）	歧（歧視）
昌（許昌）	肯（不肯）	撿（撿起）	枝（樹枝）

訂（制訂）	厢（車厢）	躍（活躍）	烈（激烈）
定（決定）	相（相信）	妖（妖精）	列（排列）

詞語運用

見聞

你這次旅行有什麼有趣的見聞？快給我們說一說吧。

激烈

大家對這個問題有各種不同的意見，爭論得十分激烈。

近義詞

開端——開頭——開始　　　以往——以前——過去

回答問題

1. 忽必烈為什麼重用漢人？

2. 忽必烈怎樣推行漢法？

3. 元代海外貿易和東西方文化交流的情況是怎樣的？請具體說一說。

4. 元代文化中哪一類藝術最有成就？請舉出兩個例子。

詞語解釋

户口——住户和人口；本地區居民的身份。

空前——以前所没有。

見聞——見到和聽到的。

元曲——元朝的一種戲曲形式。

激烈——（動作、言論等）劇烈。

其次——第二；順序較後。

閱讀

馬可·波羅

馬可·波羅是意大利人，出生在威尼斯一個商人家庭。他是一個了不起的旅行家，是第一個把地大物博的中國介紹給歐洲的人。在他的《馬可·波羅遊記》中，記載了中國40多個城市，還把當時中國的自然和社會情況作了詳細的描述，例如：養蠶、絲綢、造紙、紙幣、印刷、宮殿、都城、政府以及蒙古大汗忽必烈的節慶、遊獵活動等等。

馬可·波羅像

1260年，馬可·波羅的父親和叔父經商到過中國，見過大汗忽必烈。1271年，他的父親和叔父再次動身去中國，帶著馬可·波羅同行。這次他們三人穿越西亞各國和中亞大沙漠，翻越世界屋脊帕米爾高原進入新疆，又在無邊無際的沙漠中前行。他們一路歷經千辛萬苦，有時候一連十幾天遇不到一户人家，空中見不到一隻飛鳥，路上看不到一棵青草。就這樣，他們用了三年半的時間終於到達了上都(dū)（今內蒙古多倫縣），見到了元世祖忽必烈。

忽必烈見到他們非常高興，設宴歡迎他們，並留他們居住下來。馬可·波羅聰明好學，很快學會了蒙古語和漢語。忽必烈很信任他，除了讓他在大都工作外，還派他到國內各地和一些鄰近國家進行訪問。他到過中國的大部分地區，從運河乘船去過江

南。據說他還在揚州當過官。

轉眼，馬可·波羅和父親、叔父在中國已經生活了17年。他們想回家鄉威尼斯看看。正巧元世祖的一位公主要遠嫁到伊兒汗國，他讓馬可·波羅父子三人護送公主從海上去，但要求他們送到以後再返回中國。馬可·波羅父子帶著忽必烈寫給法國、英國和西班牙等國國王的書信，帶領十四艘船出發了。他們用了兩年半的時間纔到達了伊兒汗國。之後，他們想回家看看，但是在回鄉的路上聽到元世祖去世的消息，後來就沒有再回到中國。

公元1295年，馬可·波羅回到了家鄉威尼斯。當時威尼斯正在打仗，馬可·波羅加入了威尼斯軍隊，在作戰中被俘。在監獄裏，他和一位作家關在一起。他把中國的故事講給作家聽，經過作家記錄、整理，寫出了著名的《馬可·波羅遊記》。

《馬可·波羅遊記》七百多年來在世界各地流傳，譯本超過了一百種。馬可·波羅的著作對於人們瞭解亞洲的歷史、地理，以及中西交通的歷史，起了很大的作用。

馬可·波羅旅行路線圖

生詞

liǎo bu qǐ 了不起	great; extraordinary	xìn rèn 信任	trust
shū fù 叔父	uncle	zhèng qiǎo 正 巧	just in time; happen to
wū jǐ 屋脊	ridge of a roof	gōng zhǔ 公 主	princess
pà mǐ ěr gāoyuán 帕米爾高原	Pamir Mountain Area	zhěng lǐ 整 理	arrange; collate

English Translation

Lesson 15

The Yuan Empire

Kublai Khan founded the Mongolian Yuan Dynasty, the first minority state power ruling the entire country in the history of China. The territory of the Yuan Empire is ranked the first among all dynasties, and Kublai Khan was an outstanding emperor who realized clearly that what lay behind the impressive military achievements of Genghis Khan was the lack of experience in administration and the backward understanding the Mongolians had with regards to life issues. Therefore, he appointed Han officials to take important posts and promoted the laws and culture of Han empire extensively. This in turn helped the Yuan Empire in achieving great progress.

In order to manage a country with such vast territory, the Yuan government established the system of administrative provinces, where the central secretariat was to be in charge of national affairs, while local executive secretariats (known as executive provinces or provinces) were led by officials directly appointed by the emperor to be in charge of local affairs. With this system, the remote regions were as well administrated by the state as inland areas were and they paid their due duties and taxes to the central government too.

During the Yuan Dynasty, today's Tibet was the official executive area of the Yuan Government where officials checked and registered permanent residence and collected taxes. In A.D. 1360, the Penghu Inspection Office was established to administrate the Penghu Islands and Liuqiu (today's Taiwan).

Kublai Khan also adopted policies in favor of farmers to recover and develop agriculture. Mongolia used to be a nomadic country, but after they occupied the agricultural area along the Yellow River, the Mongolians drove the Han locals away and let the grass grow and livestock roam in the fields. But Kublai Khan ordered to protect the agriculture and to retain farming lands. He established an Agriculture Development Office for the purpose of the development and promotion of agricultural production by, for example, persuading farmers to cultivate fields, plant mulberry trees, and rear silkworms.

Kublai Khan advocated the traditional culture of the Han nationality which centered on Confucianism. He was profoundly influenced by Confucianism when he was young and often invited Confucian scholars to discuss about Confucian theories. When he became the emperor, he ordered the construction of Confucian temples, the restoration of academies, the establishment of the Imperial Academy, and the education of the children of Mongolian officials and officers with the Han culture. Thanks to Kublai Khan's active promotion of laws adapted from the Han culture, the humble kingdom of Mongolia which had originated from the grassland areas finally evolved into the great Yuan Dynasty.

Overseas trade prospered significantly in the Mid-Yuan Dynasty. Due to smooth communication between the east and the west, business activities carried out between Europe and Asia were vibrant and thriving. Businessmen passed on the printing technique and gunpowder from China to the west and China was, at the same time, introduced to western culture. Many foreign businessmen and envoys sought after long-term stay in Beijing. Italian traveler Marco Polo wrote a book entitled *The Travels of Marco Polo* and this book caused a stir in Europe. In the book, he talked about his 17-year experience in China and since then the Europeans grew in awareness about China. Moreover, the flourishing seaborne trade, inland water transport and business, as well as the circulation of paper money made the Yuan Dynasty one of the most populous and richest countries in the world.

Both technology and art achieved great progress during the Yuan Dynasty. According to the Shoushi Calendar invented by astronomer Guo Shoujing, there were 365.2425 days in a year, and this calculation matches the current Gregorian calendar exactly. There were many cotton textile manufacturers and traders during this period of time in China, among all of whom Huang Daopo was most famous. She improved and promoted the use of the spinning wheel, the weaving machine, and the cotton textile technique which resulted in a large amount of cotton cloth output in China. Yuan Qu, a verse form popular in the Yuan Dynasty, served as the origin of Chinese modern opera, and its masterpieces included *Injustice to Dou E by* Guan Hanqing and *Romance of the West Chamber* by Wang Shifu.

The Yuan government, however, adopted policies of national discrimination and oppression in order to maintain the status of the Mongolian nobles. The Yuan government divided the national population into four grades, with the Mongolian race being the most revered, followed by the Semu people, then the people of Han nationality, and lastly the Southern people. The last two grades of the Han and Southern people were discriminated against in politics, laws, and imperial examinations. These policies were unpopular and caused the intensification of national conflicts. After Kublai Khan died, his descendents fought bitterly for the throne. This, together with the widespread yet unsolved famine due to crop failures for years, initiated the Red-Turban Rebelling. The leader of the uprising, Zhu Yuanzhang, came to the throne in A.D. 1368 in today's Nanjing and founded the Ming Dynasty. However the insurrectionists seized the capital city of Dadu in the very same year and the Yuan Dynasty came to the end.

Marco Polo

Marco Polo was an Italian and was born into a businessman family in Venice. He was a great traveler and the first person who introduced China to Europe as a country with vast territory and rich resources. In *The Travels of Marco Polo*, he recorded his travels in more than 40 Chinese cities, describing in detail both the natural and social information of China at that time, for example: silkworms rearing, silk products, paper making, printing, palaces, capital city, government, the festivals, as well as Kublai Khan's hunting activities.

In A.D. 1260, Marco Polo's father and uncle traveled to China on business and met up with Kublai Khan. In A.D. 1271, his father and uncle paid another visit to China, bringing Marco Polo along with them. This time, the three of them came across the West Asia and the desert in Middle Asia, and entered Xinjiang through the Pamir Mountain Area, the world ridge, before conquering the vast desert. They went through many difficulties along the way and could hardly see a household, or a flying bird in sky, or a green grass on their way for dozens of days. It took them three and a half years to reach Shangdu (today's Duolun County in Inner Mongolia) and meet Kublai Khan, Emperor Shizu of the Yuan Dynasty.

Kublai Khan was happy to meet them, and treated them to banquets, asking them to stay. Marco Polo was smart and diligent and soon learned both languages of the Mongolians and the Chinese. Kublai Khan trusted him and apart from offering him jobs inside Dadu, he sent Marco Polo to visit other domestic places and surrounding countries. Therefore, Marco traveled to many places in China and visited the southern area of the lower reaches of the Yangtze River on boat through the Grand Canal. It is said that he once served as a local official in Yangzhou.

Time passed quickly and Marco Polo, together with his father and uncle, had lived in China for 17 years. They wanted to go back to their hometown in Venice. Emperor Shizu of the Yuan Dynasty planned to marry one of his princesses to the Kingdom of Il-Khan, so he ordered that Marco Polo, his father, and uncle escort the princess on her seaborne journey on the condition that they return to China once the mission was accomplished. The three of them went on the journey with 14 boats and the letters written by Kublai Khan for the kings of France, Great Britain, and Spain. It took them two and a half years to arrive at the destination. Then they wanted to drop by their hometown and on their way there, they received the news that Emperor Shizu of the Yuan Dynasty passed away. They never went back to China upon hearing this news.

In A.D. 1295, Marco Polo came back to his hometown Venice, which was engaged in war at that time, and he joined the army. After being caught in a battle and thrown into prison, Marco Polo met a cellmate who was a writer. He told the writer stories about China and the writer recorded what he said and composed the well-known *The Travels of Marco Polo*.

The Travels of Marco Polo became popular in the world for more than 700 years and was translated into over 100 different languages, contributing a great deal of information for people to understand the history and geography of Asia, as well as the long history of communication between China and the West.

第十六課

明（上）

明朝的第一個皇帝朱元璋(zhāng)，出身貧苦，做過和尚，後來參加元末紅巾軍起義，成為義軍領袖，並於公元1368年在今南京建立明朝。他就是明太祖。

鄭和寶船圖

明朝建國後，朱元璋把兒子們分封到各地去做藩(fān)王，他們都帶領著很多軍隊，其中燕(yān)王朱棣(dì)的軍力最強。朱元璋死後把皇位傳給了孫子建文帝。因為建文帝年紀很小，燕王朱棣起兵造反。公元1402年，他趕走建文帝，自己做了皇帝，並把首都從南京遷到了北京。

朱棣是一位胸懷大志的帝王，在他的統治下，明朝越來越強大。他曾派太監鄭和帶領船隊出使西洋①。鄭和的遠航不僅使明朝的威望提高，促進了中外文化交流，而且激起了中國人向海外

---

① 西洋——當時把中國南海以西的海洋稱為西洋。

發展的興趣。從此廣東、福建移民南洋的人漸漸多了起來。

北京成為明朝的首都以後，幾百年來一直是中國政治、經濟和文化的中心。

北京故宮

北京的城市建築佈局嚴整，城牆高大雄偉，街道寬闊筆直，是古代城市建築的傑作。城市中心為皇宮，金碧輝煌，是現今世界上最大、保留最完整的古代宮殿建築群。明朝又修復了長城。明長城東起山海關①，西到嘉峪關②，全長6,000多千米，修復工程浩大。

青花束蓮盤（明）

明初的政策是減輕人民的稅賦，恢復和發展生產。很快，明朝農業的產量就遠遠超過了前代。農村多餘的勞動力流入了手工業與商業，使手工業和商業發展起來。當時的手工業技術十分精巧，生產規模也不斷擴大，出現了雇傭關係。例如，明朝的青花

① 山海關——地名，在今河北省秦皇島市。

② 嘉峪關——地名，在今甘肅省嘉峪關市。

瓷十分精美，聞名於世。生產瓷器的景德鎮，幾十里內，處處有窯，雇工成百上千。經過景德鎮的道路、河流沿途盡是運送瓷器的車船。當時的絲綢更是花色繁多。明朝中葉以後，江南蘇杭地區絲織業特別發達，城鎮居民無論男女老幼，大多進入絲織業。富人為雇主，雇有長工和短工，大的作坊有幾十臺織機。精美的瓷器和絲綢是中國主要的出口商品，銷售到歐洲和美洲，換取了大量的白銀。那時候，明朝在國際貿易中獲得的是順差。

明人演戲圖

明朝的時候，中國的傳統科學技術仍然處於世界領先的地位。當時的科學家寫出了三部科學巨著：《本草綱目》、《農政全書》和《天工開物》。《本草綱目》是著名藥物學家、醫學家李時珍用27年時間完成的一部藥物學巨著，是當時世界上內容最豐富、最詳細的藥物學文獻。《農政全書》是科學家徐光啓寫的一部農業百科全書。它記載了中國古代有關農業的理論，並總結了中國的農田水利技術，還首次介紹了西方的農業

徐光啓像

科學知識。徐光啓不但知識廣博，而且善於學習外來的先進科學知識。他和意大利傳教士利瑪（mǎ）竇[①]一起翻譯了西方數學著作《幾何原本》，這是中國歷史上第一部科技譯著。《天工開物》是宋應星編寫的，專門介紹了明代農業、手工業的生產技術：如採煤、打井的技術和紡織業使用的提花織機等。書中有大量的插圖，人們可以清楚地看到明朝手工工場生產的情景，因此，這本書被稱為“中國17世紀的工藝百科全書”。

燒瓷（選自《天工開物》）

明代是中國古典小説蓬勃發展的時期。明朝産生了許多優秀的小説，最著名的長篇小説有《三國演義》、《水滸（hǔ）傳》和《西遊記》等。當時還出現了反對封建禮教的思想家李贄（zhì）。

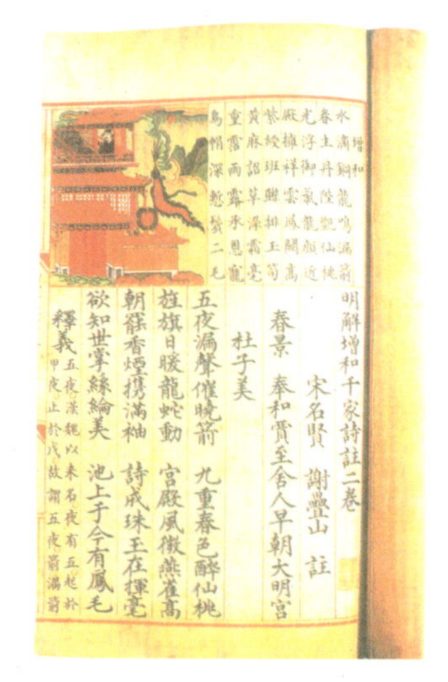
明解增和千家詩註二卷
宋名賢 謝疊山 註
春景 奉和賈至舍人早朝大明宮
杜子美
五夜漏聲催曉箭 九重春色醉仙桃
旌旗日暖龍蛇動 宮殿風微燕雀高
朝罷香煙攜滿袖 詩成珠玉在揮毫
欲知世掌絲綸美 池上于今有鳳毛
釋義

中國最早的彩印插圖書（明）

明朝是一個經濟繁榮，對外關係比較開

---

① 利瑪竇（1552—1610）——意大利人，耶穌會教士，1582年到中國傳教。他將西方的科學知識和文化傳到中國，又將中國的經典“四書”、“五經”、《道德經》等譯成拉丁文，介紹到歐洲。

放的國家。它和歐洲的文藝復興處於同一時期。明代前期，遠比西方發達，而西方到了文藝復興以後，纔趕上並超過了中國。從此，中國開始漸漸地落後了。

生詞

tài jiàn 太監	eunuch	xiāo shòu 銷售	sell
zhèng 鄭	Zheng (*surname*)	shùn chā 順差	surplus; favorable balance
bù jú 佈局	layout overall arrangement	wénxiàn 文獻	document; literature
jīn bì huī huáng 金碧輝煌	resplendent and magnificent	xú guāng qǐ 徐光啓	Xu Guangqi (*name*)
jiā yù guān 嘉峪關	Jiayu Pass	chuán jiào shì 傳教士	missionary
duō yú 多餘	spare	cǎi méi 採煤	coal mining
gù yōng 雇傭	employ; hire	gōng yì 工藝	craft; technology
yáo 窯	kiln	wén yì fù xīng 文藝復興	Renaissance (in the 14th-17th centuries in western Europe)
chéngzhèn 城鎮	cities and towns		

聽寫

徐光啓　城鎮　銷售　採煤　鄭成功　多餘　金碧輝煌

領先　沿途　胸懷大志　*廣博

比一比

領｛領袖、領導、帶領｝ 獻｛文獻、獻出｝ 城｛城鎮、城市｝ 胸｛胸懷大志、胸有成竹｝

精｛精巧、精美｝ 順｛順差、順利｝ 餘｛多餘、剩餘｝ ｛煤（採煤）、謀（謀略）｝

詞語運用

領先

比賽一開始紅隊領先，後來藍隊超過紅隊，奪取了冠軍。

多餘

我們是十個人，您給了十一雙鞋，多餘一雙，請您收回去吧。

沿途

我騎著自行車在郊外旅行，沿途的風景很美麗，我的心情也很愉快。

回答問題

1. 明朝的三部科學巨著名字是什麼？請分別説一説它們屬於哪一個學科，作者是誰。

2. 你知道明朝哪三部著名的長篇小説？請説一説它們的作者是誰。

詞語解釋

胸懷大志——心裏存著遠大的志向。

嚴整——嚴格，工整。

金碧輝煌——形容建築物異常華麗，光彩奪目。

浩大——（聲勢、規模等）巨大。

精巧——（技術、器物構造等）精細、巧妙。

精美——精巧、漂亮。

沿途——沿路。

花色繁多——花紋和顏色的品種很多。

領先——共同前進時走在最前面。比喻水平、成績等處(chǔ)於最前列。

廣博——範圍大，方面多（多指學識）。

封建禮教——使人們的思想和行為符合封建傳統的禮節和道德。

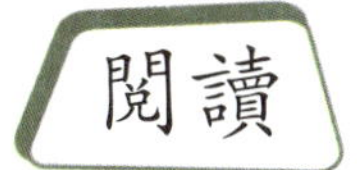
閱讀

鄭和下西洋

鄭和像

公元1405年農曆六月的一天，太平洋上風平浪靜。江蘇劉家河水面上卻是一片喧鬧，這裏整齊地排列著62條巨型海船。只聽一聲令下，十幾里長的船隊浩浩盪盪，揚帆南下。帶領這只船隊的是三寶太監鄭和。

明朝前期的“與民休息”政策使經濟快速增長，中國成了亞洲最富強的國家。當時，中國的紡織、陶瓷製造、造船、航海業都處於世界領先的地位。明成祖是一位思想比較開放的皇帝，他派太監鄭和率船隊出使西洋各國，提高了中國的威望，促進了國際貿易的往來。

鄭和原來姓馬，回族人，公元1371年出生在雲南。鄭和第一次下西洋時，他的船隊共有27,000多人，除水手、官兵之外，還有工匠、醫生、翻譯等。他們的船稱為寶船，最大的長約138米，寬56米，可容納1,000人，是當時世界上最大的海船。船隊之大，

也是當時世界上獨一無二的。公元1492年哥倫布首次遠航時，他的船隊僅有3艘船（船長18米）和90名水手。

鄭和帶著國書，每到一國都會和當地的君主會面，宣讀國書，贈送珍貴禮物，表示願意建立友好關係，還熱情邀請當地國王訪問中國。同時船隊也與當地進行貿易活動，用中國的金銀、絲綢、瓷器等物品換回珠寶、香料和藥材。鄭和的遠航加強了明朝同各國的友好關係。那時候蘇祿等國的國王、王子都來過中國。隨鄭和前來的使節、商人更是多達上千人。公元1435年，鄭和在最後一次出使西洋的歸途中死在他鄉。

鄭和是世界歷史上最傑出的航海家之一。鄭和七次下西洋，前後 28年。他的船隊到過亞洲和非洲的30多個國家和地區，最遠到達了今天的紅海一帶和非洲東海岸。直到今天，南洋群島和印度洋一些地區還保存著紀念鄭和的石碑和廟宇。可是，自從鄭和死後，中國人的身影就消失在海上了。

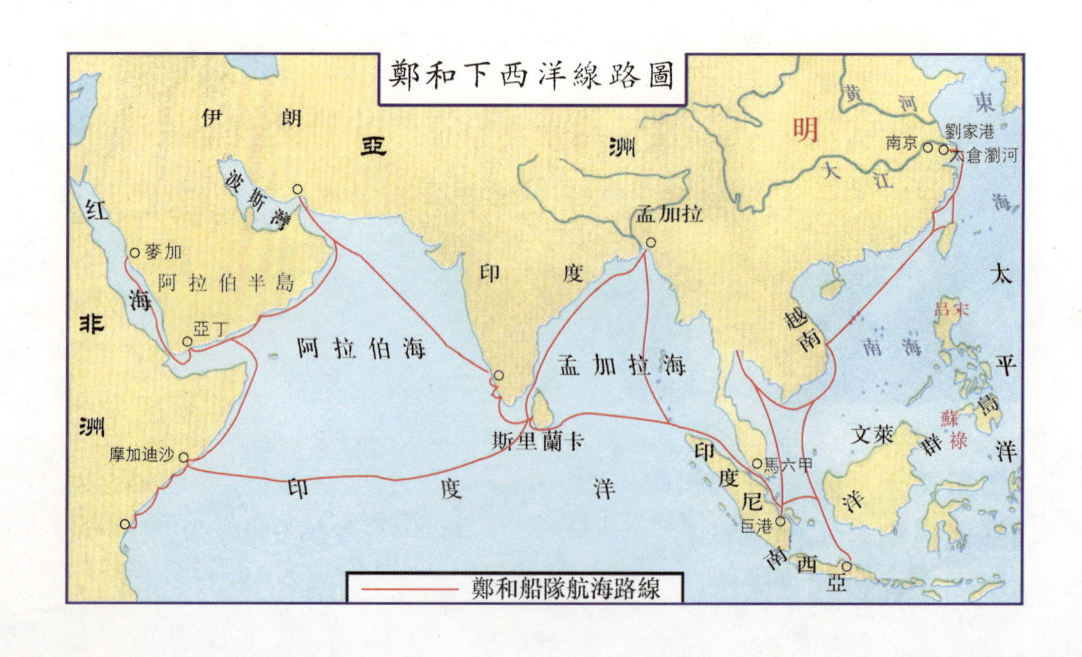

生詞

xuān nào 喧鬧	noise and excitemert	sū lù 蘇禄	Sulu
yáng fān 揚帆	set sail	tā xiāng 他鄉	alien land; a place for away from home
róng nà 容納	have a capacity of	hóng hǎi 紅海	the Red Sea
gē lún bù 哥倫布	Christopher Columbus	miào yǔ 廟宇	temple
guó shū 國書	letter of credence	shēnyǐng 身影	figure; a person's silhouette
zèngsòng 贈送	present		

譯文 *English Translation*

Lesson 16

Ming (Ⅰ)

Zhu Yuanzhang, the first emperor of the Ming Dynasty, was born in a poor family and used to be a monk. He then joined the Red-Turban Rebelling at the end of the Yuan Dynasty and became a leader. He founded the Ming Dynasty in A.D. 1368 in today's Nanjing and became Emperor Taizu of the Ming Dynasty.

After founding the Ming Dynasty, Zhu Yuanzhang sent his sons to be seigniors in different places and they all led their own armies, among which the one led by Zhu Di in Yan was the strongest. Before his death, Zhu Yuanzhang passed his throne to his grandson Emperor Jianwen. Emperor Jianwen, however, was very young at the time and Zhu Di, the seignior of Yan, rebelled and came to the throne himself in A.D. 1402 by driving Emperor Jianwen away. He then moved the capital from Nanjing to Beijing.

Zhu Di was an ambitious emperor and the Ming Dynasty became increasingly powerful under his rule. He used to send Zheng He, a eunuch, and a fleet on diplomatic missions to the west. Zheng He's amazing skills of navigation not only improved the Ming government's reputation, but also promoted cultural exchanges between China and the West, and this initiated the Chinese's interest in overseas development. Eventually, more and more people migrated from Guangdong and Fujian to other parts of Southeast Asia.

Beijing, the capital city of Ming, has been the political, economic, and cultural center of China for several hundred years. The architecture of Beijing city was neatly arranged, with grand city walls, wide and straight streets, and it was regarded as the masterpiece of all other city construction in ancient times. The entire city centered on the resplendent and magnificent imperial palace. It is the largest and the best preserved ancient palace building in the world. The Ming government renovated the Great Wall from the Shanhai Pass in the east to the Jiayu Pass in the west with a total length of over 6,000 kilometers, making it a huge project.

The policy adopted in the early Ming Dynasty was to reduce tax, recover and develop the country's production. It was not long when the agricultural output during the Ming Dynasty far exceeded that of the previous dynasties. The input of rural laborers contributed to the rapid growth of the handicraft industry and business. The handicraft techniques during that time were extremely exquisite, and its production scale saw continuous expansion, resulting in the start of employment system. For example, the blue and white porcelain produced during the Ming Dynasty was extremely famous worldwide. In Jingde Town, where most of its business was dedicated to the production of porcelain, one will be able to see furnaces everywhere within the area of dozens of *li* and tens of hundreds of employees hard at work. Vehicles and boats loaded with porcelain products could be found everywhere on the roads and in rivers passing through the town. The silk products at that time were extremely rich in variety. After the Mid-Ming Dynasty, the silk textile industry began its development in Suzhou and Hangzhou, and almost all residents, regardless of sex and age, joined the craze for silk textile. The rich employed and hired both long-term and short-term laborers. There were dozens of weaving machines in large work-shops. Exquisite porcelain and silk products were the main commodities that China exported to Europe and America for large amounts of silver. At that time, the Ming government enjoyed advantages from international trade and received much revenue.

During the Ming Dynasty, traditional Chinese science and technology still took the foremost position in the world. The Ming scientists produced three important scientific works: *Compendium of Materia Medica* (*Bencao Gangmu*), *Complete Treatise on Agricultural Administration* (*Nongzheng Quanshu*), and *Exploitation of the Works of Nature* (*Tiangong Kaiwu*). The *Compendium of Materia Medica* is a great book on pharmacology written by a famous pharmacologist and medical scientist, Li Shizhen, in which he summarized his 27-year experience in the field. The book is a pharmacological literature with the richest and the most detailed content on pharmacology in the world at that time. The *Complete Treatise on Agricultural Administration* is an agricultural encyclopedia written by scientist Xu Guangqi which records ancient Chinese theories on agriculture, summarizes Chinese water conservancy technologies for farming, and introduces for the first time western scientific agricultural knowledge. Xu Guangqi was very knowledgeable and could understand advanced foreign sciences easily and quickly. He cooperated with Matteo Ricci, an Italian Jesuit Missionary, in translating Euclid's *Elements* on western mathematics literature, the first translation work ever done on science and technology. The *Exploitation of the Works of Nature* written by Song Yingxing focuses on production

technologies of the agriculture and handicraft industries during the Ming Dynasty, such as coal mining, well digging, and the jacquard loom used in textile industry. There are many illustrations in his book and this is to allow readers to have a better understanding of the production scenes in these workshops. The book has been famed as the "Encyclopedia on Technologies of China" in the 17th century.

Chinese classical novels flourished during the Ming Dynasty and there were a lot of masterpieces during the period, including *The Romance of Three Kingdoms*, *Outlaws of the Marsh*, and *Journey to the West*. There was also a famous thinker Li Zhi at that time who was against feudal ethical codes.

Generally, China enjoyed a prosperous economy and relatively open foreign policies during the Ming Dynasty. This was also the Renaissance period in Europe. In the early Ming Dynasty, China was much more developed than the western countries. After the Renaissance period in Europe, however, the west caught up with China. From then on, China began to decline gradually.

Zheng He's Expedition to the West

It was July 1405. The Pacific Ocean was calm and peaceful. However, the Liujiahe River of Jiangsu was bustling with activity, for 62 massive sea boats were neatly arranged there. At an order, the entire fleet of them which stretched to about a dozen *li* long set sail and headed south. Zheng He, Eunuch Sanbao, led the fleet.

The policy of rehabilitation was adopted in the early Ming Dynasty and this led to the rapid growth of the national economy, and China eventually became the most powerful country in Asia. At that time, China was the worldwide leader in the textile industry, porcelain production, shipbuilding, and navigation. Emperor Chengzu of the Ming Dynasty was an open-minded man and he sent a fleet led by Zheng He on a diplomatic mission to the west in order to promote China's reputation and encourage international business and exchanges.

Zheng He's original surname was Ma, and he was born of Hui nationality in A.D. 1371 in Yunnan. During the first expedition to the west, his fleet had more than 27,000 men, including sailors, officials, soldiers, craftsmen, doctors, and interpreters. Their boats were known as Treasure Ships. The largest boat was 138 meters long and 56 meters wide, and it was capable of holding 1,000 people. It was also the largest sea boat in the world and the fleet was also the largest fleet that ever set sail at that time. When Columbus started his first journey in A.D. 1492, he led a fleet of merely three boats that were 18 meters long with 90 sailors.

Zheng He brought letters of credence along with him and met the local monarch each time his fleet arrived at a country. He would then read the letter to the monarch and present precious gifts to show China's sincerity in maintaining good relationships with their countries, and invite the local monarchs to visit China. At the same time, his fleet also did business with the local people, exchanging jewelries, spices, and herbs with gold, silver, silk, and porcelain. Zheng He's expedition reinforced the friendly relationships between the Ming government with other countries. At that time, the kings and princes of Sulu and other countries paid visits to China and more than 1,000 envoys and businessmen came to China with Zheng He. In A.D. 1435, Zheng He died in a foreign country on his way back to

China from his last mission to the west.

Zheng He was indeed one of the most outstanding navigators in the history of world. He visited the west for seven times in 28 years and his fleet traveled to more than 30 countries and areas in Asia and Africa, reaching as far as today's Red Sea and to the African east coast. As of today, there are still stone monuments and temples commemorating Zheng He in some parts of the Southeast Asian islands and Indian Ocean. But after his death, all traces of the Chinese people disappeared from the vast sea.

第十七課

明（下）

明朝的滅亡

明朝中後期，宦官專權，政治腐敗。皇親國戚佔有大量土地和財富。農民們失去土地和房屋，缺少衣服和食物，成為“流民”。那個時期，全國的流民多達幾百萬人。公元1627年，陝西農民的起義爆發了。公元1636年，起義軍的一個首領李自成，被衆人推舉為“闖王”，成為起義軍的領袖。當時起義軍面臨官軍的鎮壓，處境艱難。但是李自成堅持鬥爭，隊伍迅速發展壯大。他還提出了“均田免糧”的口號，得到廣大農民的擁護，起義軍很快發展到數十萬人。李自成於公元1643年建立大順朝。

明朝皇后鳳冠

《鐵冠圖》（清末年畫——崇禎賜死皇后，然後自殺）

公元1644年，李自成帶領起義軍攻入北京，明朝皇帝在煤山（今北京景山）自殺，明朝滅亡。

李自成進入北京之後，明朝大將吴三桂投降清軍，聯合清軍一起攻打起義軍。李自成在山海關被打敗，匆忙退出北京城。清軍緊追不捨，李自成最後戰死於湖北。李自成從進入北京到撤離，前後僅僅41天。

清軍佔領北京以後，把首都遷到北京，開始了對全國的統治。

民族英雄鄭成功

鄭成功是抗清名將，也是收復台灣的民族英雄。開始，鄭成功以廈門為根據地，起兵抗清。他的隊伍不斷壯大，曾率領十萬大軍進攻南京。北伐失敗以後，他的軍隊退回到廈門，準備驅逐

鄭成功收復台灣

荷蘭人，收復台灣，以台灣為抗清的基地。公元1661年鄭成功帶領2.5萬名將士和數百艘戰船，向台灣進軍。經過八個月的戰鬥，於公元1662年打敗荷蘭人，收復了台灣。

鄭成功收復台灣後，下令讓幾萬士兵和隨軍家屬開荒種田。不久，在台灣南部和西部的彰化、新竹等地逐漸形成了一大批村鎮。

收復台灣不久， 鄭成功因病身亡，年僅38歲。他的兒子鄭經、孫子鄭克塽前後治理台灣22年。鄭氏祖孫三代治理台灣時，獎勵製糖、製鹽，興辦工商業，發展貿易，開辦學堂，改進高山族的農業生產方式。這些都推動了台灣經濟、文化的發展。在台灣歷史上，這是一個重要的開發和發展時期，史稱“明鄭時代”。

公元1683年，清政府派軍進攻台灣，鄭克塽率衆歸順。自此台灣在清政府直接統治之下，屬福建省。

十色紙（明朝紙的顏色豐富，多用植物染料染色）

生詞

huàn guān 宦官	eunuch		qū zhú 驅逐	drive out; expel
huáng qīn guó qì 皇親國戚	imperial family and their relatives		hé lán 荷蘭	Netherland
cái fù 財富	fortune		jī dì 基地	base
chǔ jìng 處境	(*unfavorable*) situation		jiā shǔ 家屬	family dependents; family members
zhuàng dà 壯大	strengthen; family members		zhāng huà 彰化	Zhanghua (*place*)
cōng máng 匆忙	in a hurry		zhì lǐ 治理	govern
shōu fù 收復	recover		guī shùn 歸順	come over and pledge allegiance
xià mén 廈門	Xiamen (*place*)			

聽寫

廈門　親戚　壯大　家屬　荷蘭　財富　匆忙

收復　基地　*驅逐　處境

比一比

宦（宦官）	荷（荷蘭）	廈（廈門）	彰（彰化）
臣（大臣）	何（如何）	夏（夏天）	章（文章）
驅（驅逐）	財（財富）	匆（匆忙）	
區（區別）	才（人才）	勿（請勿入内）	

詞語運用

匆（匆）忙（忙）

鄭先生的時間總是不夠用，幹什麼都是匆匆忙忙的。

近義詞

收復——奪回　　投降——歸順　　宦官——太監

回答問題

1. 明末農民起義的傑出領袖是誰?

2. 鄭成功從哪國人的手中收復了台灣?

3. 鄭成功哪一年收復了台灣?

詞語解釋

緊追不捨 —— 緊緊追趕，不肯放弃。

閱讀

利瑪(mǎ)竇

16世紀新航路開辟後，歐洲的一些天主教傳教士來中國傳教，其中最有名的是利瑪竇。

利瑪竇（1552—1610）是意大利人，耶穌會教士，1582年到中國傳教。他努力學習漢語，瞭解中國的風土人情，一兩年以後，便可以閱讀中國經典了。1585年，他建立了中國內地的第一座天主教堂。

利瑪竇像

利瑪竇很有學問，他精通“四書五經”，尊重中國文化，允許教徒祭孔祭祖，因而得到了中國人的信任和友誼。後來，明朝皇帝接見了他，特許他在北京建教堂傳教。那時中國人對天主教很陌生，傳教並不容易。他不但向中國人介紹西方的宗教和倫理學，還將西方的科學技術與發明：如歐幾里得幾何學、三角學、天文學、地理學、

測量學、透視學、西方樂器等新鮮事物介紹給中國人。

利瑪竇在中國20多年，不僅把西方介紹給中國，同時他又把中國的經典“四書”、“五經”、《道德經》等譯成拉丁文，介紹到歐洲，成為第一個把孔子和儒家思想介紹給西方的人。利瑪竇在中國與西方文化交流的歷史上書寫了重要的一章。1610年，利瑪竇病逝，葬於北京。

生詞

yē sū 耶穌	Jesus	jǐ hé xué 幾何學	geometry
jì 祭	offer sacrifices to	sān jiǎo xué 三角學	trigonometry
yǒu yì 友誼	friendship	tòu shì xué 透視學	fluoroscopy
mò shēng 陌生	unfamiliar	lā dīngwén 拉丁文	Latin
lún lǐ xué 倫理學	ethics	bìng shì 病逝	die of illness

Lesson 17

Ming (II)

The End of the Ming Dynasty

In the middle and late Ming Dynasty, the eunuchs controlled the country, and corruption plagued the national politics. The imperial family and their relatives held large amounts of land and fortune, while farmers who lost their farming land and houses were in dire need of clothes and food, and became refugees. There were, at that time, a total of several million refugees in China. In A.D. 1627, farmers in Shaanxi started an uprising and in A.D. 1636, a leader named Li Zicheng was selected to be the Daring King (*Chuangwang*) and their supreme leader. Despite official oppression, he insisted on fighting back and his force grew rapidly. He proposed the reform of "the division of farming land on an equal basis and the exemption of tax in the form of grain" and this made him extremely popular among farmers. His army hence grew quickly to several hundred thousand soldiers. Eventually, Li Zicheng founded the great Shun Dynasty in A.D. 1643. In A.D. 1644, Li Zicheng led his army and seized Beijing. The emperor of the Ming Dynasty committed suicide in Coal Hill (today's Jingshan Hill in Beijing), marking the end of the Ming Dynasty.

After Li Zicheng seized Beijing, General Wu Sangui of the Ming Dynasty surrendered to Qing and joined hands with the Qing army in fighting against Li Zicheng. Li, who was overpowered, was defeated in Shanhai Pass and had to retreat from Beijing. With the Qing army pursuing behind, Li Zicheng died in a battle in Hubei, and he had ruled Beijing for only 41 days.

The Qing army seized Beijing and moved the capital of China to this city, starting its reign on China.

Zheng Chenggong, a National Hero

General Zheng Chenggong is a national hero famous for fighting against the Qing army and recovering Taiwan. Firstly, Zheng Chenggong was based on Xiamen in fighting against Qing. As his army grew, he once led 100,000 soldiers on an attack on Nanjing. When the north expedition failed, he retreated to Xiamen, and prepared for driving the Netherlanders out and recovering Taiwan so as to continue fighting with Qing. In A.D. 1661, Zheng Chenggong led 25,000 soldiers and hundreds of warships toward Taiwan. After eight months of fighting, he finally defeated the Netherlanders and recovered Taiwan in A.D. 1662.

After Taiwan's successful retrieval, Zheng Chenggong ordered his numerous soldiers and their dependants to open up the wasteland for cultivation. Soon, many villages and towns appeared in the southern and western parts of Taiwan, including Zhanghua and Xinzhu.

Shortly after recovering Taiwan, Zheng Chenggong died of illness at the age of 38. His son Zheng Jing and grandson Zheng Keshuang governed Taiwan for 22 years. Under the reign of three generations of Zhengs in Taiwan, sugar and salt production was encouraged industry, there was promotion of various industries and business, trade saw significant development, schools were built, and the agricultural production methods of local Gaoshan nationality was greatly improved. All this contributed considerably to the development of both economy and culture in Taiwan. This is an important period of development and growth in Taiwan and is known as "the Period of the Zheng Regime during the Ming Dynasty."

The Qing government sent an army to attack Taiwan in A.D. 1683 and Zheng Keshuang surrendered under the pressure. Since then, Taiwan was placed under the direct control of the Qing government and the administration of Fujian Province.

Matteo Ricci

After the development of a new navigation route in the 16th century, many European Catholic missionaries came to China. Matteo Ricci was probably the most famous among all of them.

Matteo Ricci (1552-1610) was an Italian Jesuit Missionary and arrived in China in A.D. 1582. He worked hard to learn Chinese and understand the Chinese customs and was able to read Chinese classics within a year or two. In A.D. 1585, he built the first Catholic Church in inland China.

Matteo Ricci was extremely learned. He was an expert on the *Four Books* and *Five Classics* and he respected the Chinese culture and allowed believers to worship Confucius and their ancestors which gained him the trust and friendship of the Chinese people. Later on, the emperor of the Ming Dynasty sent for him and allowed him to build a church and do missionary works in Beijing. At that time, Catholicism was strange to the Chinese people and it was not an easy task to reach out to them. He introduced the Chinese people not only to western religion and ethnics, but also to western scientific and technologic achievements, including Euclid's geometry, trigonometry, astronomy, geography, surveying, fluoroscopy, as well as other new things such as western instruments.

Apart from introducing the western world to China, Matteo Ricci also translated Chinese classic literature into Latin during his 20-year stay in China and introduced Chinese literature, which included the *Four Books*, *Five Classics*, and Laozi's *Tao Teh Ching*, to Europe. This made him the first person to introduce Confucius and Confucianism to the west. Matteo Ricci had indeed composed an important chapter in the history of cultural communication between China and the west. In A.D. 1610, Matteo Ricci died of illness and was buried in Beijing.

第十八課

清（上）

清朝是中國封建社會最後一個朝代，是由滿族人建立的。滿族在歷史上稱為女真，居住在黑龍江下游。公元1616年，努爾哈赤統一了女真部落，建立金政權（史稱後金）。公元1636年，努爾哈赤的兒子皇太極改國號為“清”。公元1644年，李自成領導的農民起義軍推翻了明朝，清軍乘機進入山海關，打敗了起義軍，定都北京。

康熙皇帝像

清朝初期實行獎勵開荒、減少稅收的政策，內地和邊疆經濟都有了發展。到18世紀中葉，清的國力強大起來，人口達3億多。

康熙皇帝是中國歷史上一位有名的皇帝。公元1683年，他出兵統一了台灣，在台灣設一府三縣，屬福建省。清軍佔領全中國，先後用了幾十年時間。在這期間，俄羅斯多次進犯中國黑龍江地區，並佔領雅克薩城。康熙皇帝兩次派兵出擊，俄軍戰敗。1689年，兩國簽訂《尼布楚條約》，劃定邊界，從此以後的一百

多年裏，中國東北十分平靜。到乾隆皇帝（康熙帝的孫子）時，最終平定了蒙古準噶爾部，統一了新疆。之後，清政府注意發展邊疆的經濟、文化和交通，鞏固了中國多民族國家的統一，清朝的疆域達到1,200萬平方千米。

故宮乾清宮

yōng
雍正皇帝（康熙帝的兒子）時，改革了稅收制度，取消了丁銀（人頭稅），只按土地收稅，減輕了人民的負擔，農業生產得到發展。

早在明朝時，中國與西方國家之間，不僅商貿活動頻繁，而且文化交流也有所增加。1582年，意大利傳教士利瑪竇等已來到中國傳教。後來，日耳曼人湯若望等陸續來華。傳教士來到

中國，帶來了西方的科學知識，比如數學、天文學、地理學。同時，傳教士本身也學習中國的儒學、佛學。不過，羅馬教皇禁止中國教徒祭孔祭祖，這觸及到中國傳統文化的根本，因此，清朝時康熙皇帝下令禁止中國人信天主教。

《萬國來朝圖》局部（清）

從康熙到乾隆三代，國家穩定，社會繁榮，被稱為"康乾盛世"。但是，大清國以天朝上國自居，並未覺察世界的另一邊正發生著翻天覆地的巨大變化。歐洲人通過遠洋航行開辟了海外市場，商業經濟快速取代了農業經濟；歐洲的工業革命帶來了全新的生產方式和巨大的社會變化；科學實證代替了神學教條；民主、法制、契約的思想和制度代替了專制王權的思想和制度，法國、美國建立了民主政權，人民開始用選票治理自己的國家。這一切是那麼新鮮而有活力，西方國家正大步前進。而大清國，在經濟上依然是以農業立國，文化上提倡封建禮教，甚至大興"文字獄"①。清政府這種閉關自守、盲目自大、不思進取的做法，致使中國落後於世界的先進潮流。

① 文字獄——統治者故意從詩文中摘取字句製造罪名，迫害知識分子。

生詞

chéng jī 乘機	seize the opportunity		chù jí 觸及	touch
kāng xī 康熙	Emperor Kangxi		zì jū 自居	claim oneself to be
qiāndìng 簽訂	conclude and sign		jué chá 覺察	perceive
huàdìng 劃定	delimit; demarcate		mín zhǔ 民主	democracy
qiánlóng 乾隆	Emperor Qianlong		qì yuē 契約	contract
zhǔn gá ěr 準噶爾	Junggar (*place*)		zhuān zhì 專制	autocratic
fù dān 負擔	burden		yǐ zhì （以）致	as a result
rì ěr màn 日耳曼	Teutonic; German		cháo liú 潮流	current; tide; trend
jì kǒng 祭孔	worship Confucius			

聽寫

乘機　簽訂　負擔　覺察　民主　（以）致　法制

日耳曼　自大　潮流　*翻天覆地　祭孔

比一比

乘	乘機 乘法	簽	簽訂 簽字	覆	翻天覆地 覆蓋	祭(祭孔) 際(國際)
負	負擔 負責	覺	覺察 覺得	盲	盲目 盲人	致(以致) 至(甚至)

詞語運用

自大

驕傲自大的人往往會失敗。

負擔

做作業是為了鞏固課堂學習的知識，但是作業不能太多，否則學生負擔太重。

回答問題

1. 清朝是由哪一個民族建立的？它是中國封建社會最後一個朝代嗎？

2. 清朝時，中國為什麼落後於世界先進的潮流？

詞語解釋

教徒——信仰某種宗教的人。

翻天覆地——形容變化巨大，而且是根本的改變。

實證——實際的證明。

神學教條——宗教上的信條，信徒只能相信、服從，不能批評、懷疑。

閉關自守——閉塞關口，不跟外界往來。

盲目自大——毫無根據地自以為了不起，看不起別人。

不思進取——没有進步的願望。

閱讀

四庫全書

清朝的文化思想，一方面提倡儒家禮教，打壓一切反清言行和文字，另一方面，康乾時期，由官方組織大批學者編寫了《四庫全書》和《康熙字典》等許多書籍。

《四庫全書》由乾隆皇帝親自主持，於1773年在北京開始編寫，光是參加編寫的學者就多達500人，再加上抄寫者，共計3,800人。

編寫《四庫全書》的學者和官員們，首先在全國收集各種珍藏書籍，然後又細心整理和恢復了500多種珍貴文獻。經過十年的努力，全書共收集了3,400多種，79,000多卷，36,304冊書，為後人保留了許多珍貴的書籍和資料。《四庫全書》是封建社會官方修訂的最大叢書。

文津閣中的《四庫全書》

《四庫全書》編成後，抄成七份，分別藏於北京故宮和江浙等地的藏書樓中。其中，江浙的藏書樓對公衆開放，供各地文人查閱。

清末和民國初期，由於連年戰火，

《四庫全書》大部分遺失，留存本現存在台灣和北京圖書館。

《四庫全書》的編寫，雖有保存珍貴文獻的作用，但也是一次文化清查。一些所謂的反清書籍被銷毀了，數量達2,400多種。

琺琅彩雙聯瓶（清）

生詞

guānfāng 官方	by the government; offcial	yí shī 遺失	lose
cè 册	volume	liú cún běn 留存本	the remain books
xiū dìng 修訂	revise	wén huà qīng chá 文化清查	a thorough inspection on cultural heritages
cóng shū 叢書	series of books		
gōng zhòng 公衆	general public	xiāo huǐ 銷毀	destroy by burning

Lesson 18

Qing (I)

The Qing Dynasty is the last feudal dynasty in the history of China which was founded by the Man nationality, known in history as Nuzhen. They lived in the lower reaches of Heilongjiang River. Nurhachi unified the entire Nuzhen tribe in A.D. 1616 and founded the regime of Jin (known in history as Later Jin). In A.D. 1636, Huangtaiji, one of Nurhachi's son, changed the name of Nuzhen to Qing. In A.D. 1644, Li Zicheng led an uprising with the farmers and overthrew the Ming government. The Qing army then took the opportunity by going beyond the Shanhai Pass to defeat Li Zicheng. They finally seized the capital city of Beijing.

In the early Qing Dynasty, the government encouraged people to open up the wasteland areas for cultivation by cutting taxes, and this resulted in the economic growth in both the inland and border areas. In the mid 18th century, China had become a strong country with a total population of more than 300 million.

Emperor Kangxi is a famous emperor in the history of China. He unified Taiwan in A.D. 1683 and established a government office and three counties in Taiwan under the Fujian Province administration. It took the Qing government a couple dozen years to take hold of the entire China. During this period of time, Russia invaded the Heilongjiang area several times and took over Yakesa city. Emperor Kangxi sent an army to fight with the Russians twice and he finally defeated them. In A.D. 1689, two countries signed the *Nerchinsk Treaty* to clarify their borders and China won peace in its northwest area for more than 100 years. Under the reign of Emperor Qianlong (the grandson of Emperor Kangxi), Xinjiang was unified by the controlling of the Mongolian Junggar tribe. The Qing government emphasized also on the development of economy, culture, and communication in the border areas, and focused on the unification of this multi-national country. The total area of the territory during the Qing Dynasty was 12 million square kilometers.

Emperor Yongzheng (the son of Emperor Kangxi) reformed the taxation system and cancelled silver levied on the person (poll tax), and collected land-based tax instead as this would reduce the burden on people. This eventually resulted in the growth of agricultural production.

Business activities between China and the western countries were active as early as during the Ming Dynasty and cultural exchanges between both territories also grew considerably. In A.D. 1582, Italian missionaries including the famous Matteo Ricci came to China to convert and reach out to the people, and they were later followed by Johann Adam Schall von Bell, a German missionary. These missionaries came to China and brought with them western scientific knowledge concerning mathematics, astronomy, and geography. Meanwhile, they also learned about Chinese customs, such as Confucianism and Buddhism. But since the Catholic Pope forbade Chinese believers to worship Confucius and ancestors which would violate the root of traditional Chinese culture, Emperor Kangxi of the Qing Dynasty ordered that no Chinese was allowed to believe in Catholicism.

China enjoyed stability and prosperity under the reign of the three emperors from Kangxi to Qianlong, and this period was known in history as "The Golden Age of Kang-Qian." However, due to the Qing government's complacency in considering China to be a celestial empire, little attention was paid to the happenings elsewhere and China was unaware of the tremendous and revolutionary changes that was taking place on the other side of the world. The Europeans developed their overseas markets through sea routes and quickly replaced the agricultural economy with the commercial economy, and the European Industrial Revolution brought about brand new production methods and huge social changes. Scientific demonstrations replaced theological doctrines. Democracy, a legal system, as well as the concept and system of the contract replaced absolute monarchy. The democratic system was established in both France and US, where people started to govern their own country through the means of voting. All these changes were innovative and energetic, and the western countries progressed significantly. On the contrary, under the reign of the Qing government, the Chinese economy still depended mainly on agriculture and it advocated feudal ethical codes. Literary inquisition was also still strict at that time. The Qing government shut China off from any communication with other countries, remaining blindly arrogant and refused to make any change or progress, which resulted in China lagging behind other countries.

Complete Library in Four Branches of Literature

The culture and ideology during the Qing Dynasty was a balance of two different policies. The government, on the one hand, advocated Confucian ethical codes and oppressed all other activities and literature works against Qing but on the other hand, many scholars were involved in the composition of a series of books under the reign of Emperor Kangxi and Qianlong, which includes the *Complete Library in Four Branches of Literature* (*Siku Quanshu*) and the *Kangxi Dictionary* (*Kangxi Zidian*).

Emperor Qianlong was in charge of the composition of the *Complete Library in Four Branches of Literature* himself, and the project started in A.D. 1773 in Beijing. Some 500 scholars together with copywriters participated in the project, and a total of 3,800 people were involved in it.

To start off, scholars and officials involved in the composition of the *Complete Library in Four Branches of Literature* collected books that were carefully preserved in the entire country. They then filed and restored more than 500 precious pieces of literature. After a decade, the library collected a total of 3,400 books, 79,000 chapters, and 36,304 volumes, leaving descendants with many precious books and materials. It is the largest series of books ever edited by the feudal authority.

Seven copies of the *Complete Library in Four Branches of Literature* were transcribed after the accomplishment of its composition and were stored separately in libraries located in the Forbidden City of Beijing, Jiangsu, and Zhejiang, among which those in Jiangsu and Zhejiang were open to the public for the local scholars' reference.

At the end of the Qing Dynasty and the early Republic of China, most of the copies of the *Complete Library in Four Branches of Literature* were lost due to continuous wars and the existing ones are now kept in the Taiwan and Beijing libraries.

The composition of the *Complete Library in Four Branches of Literature* served the function of preserving precious literature, but on the other hand, it was also a thorough inspection on cultural heritage, during which many books with content supposedly against the Qing government were destroyed and the total number of such books reached 2,400.

第十九課

清（下）

18世紀末，在中英貿易中，英國一直有很大的逆差。愛喝茶的英國人每年從中國進口大量茶葉，而英國的呢絨、鐘表等在中國卻銷路不好。為此，英國曾派使節訪華，想以外交手段打開中國市場，但是被乾隆皇帝拒絕了。為了改變貿易逆差，英國居然冒天下之大不韙（wěi），開始了罪惡的鴉片貿易。到了公元1838年，每年有4萬多箱鴉片賣到中國，不但老百姓深受其害，而且白銀大量外流。從公元1820年到1840年，從中國流出的白銀相當於當時大清國兩年的財政總收入。

林則徐像

鴉片戰爭海戰圖

公元1838年底，清朝皇帝命令林則徐禁煙。第二年，林則徐到達廣州之後，在虎門將收繳的鴉片全部銷毀，這就是歷史上著名的“虎門銷煙”。公元1840年，英國派軍艦入侵中國廣州和浙江，發動了“鴉片戰爭”，受到清軍奮力抵抗，英軍敗退。可是英國人轉而北上，到達天津，直逼北京。後來英軍又深入長江口，打到南京城下。公元1842年，清政府被迫同英國簽訂了中國近代史上第一個不平等條約——中英《南京條約》。條約規定：中國向英國賠償2,100萬銀圓，割讓香港島，開放五個通商口岸，以及英國單方面擁有“領事裁判權”①等。從此，中國淪為半殖民地半封建社會。

鴉片戰爭以後，英國、法國在公元1856年又發動了第二次鴉片戰爭，企圖得到更多的利益。公元1860年英法聯軍攻進北京，放火燒毀了舉世無雙的皇家園林——圓明園，清朝咸豐皇帝逃到承德。公元1861年，咸豐皇帝病死，他的貴妃聯合他的一個弟弟發動了北京政變，掌握了政權，這個貴妃就是後來的慈禧(xǐ)太后，也稱“西太后”。西太后統治的時期是清朝最黑暗和衰落的時期。她頑固守舊，反對革新。她鎮壓太

圓明園大水法遺跡

① 領事裁判權——外國人在中國犯了罪，中國法庭無權審判，只能由外國的領事來裁判。

圓明園大水法（噴泉）

平天國農民起義[1]、義和團運動[2]，並殺害了百日維新[3]的英雄譚嗣(sì)同等人；對英、法、日等國的侵略卻無力抵抗，節節敗退。

19世紀後半期的五十年中，鴉片貿易成了合法貿易。外國的入侵規模一次比一次大，對中國造成的傷害一次比一次嚴重。開始是俄國強迫清政府簽訂了《璦琿(ài huī)條約》，以後又有中法戰爭和《中法新約》，中日甲午戰爭和《馬關條約》，八國聯軍[4]侵華戰爭和《辛丑條約》等等。這些條約使中國喪失了東北和西北的150萬平方千米的土地和台灣、香港新界、大連、青島等地方，賠款總計十幾億兩白銀

---

① 太平天國農民起義——公元1851年，洪秀全領導農民起義，建立太平天國。

② 義和團運動——19世紀末，中國北方的農民和城市平民自發組織的反對帝國主義的武裝鬥爭。

③ 百日維新——又稱戊戌(wù xū)變法，是公元1898年光緒皇帝支持康有為、梁啓超等人進行的一次政治改革，僅僅103天就被慈禧太后鎮壓下去，變法失敗。

④ 八國聯軍——1900年由英、美、德、法、俄、日、意、奧八國組成的侵華聯軍。

孫中山

(包括利息)。中國遭受了前所未有的打擊，老百姓再也不能忍受下去，一場浩大的革命開始了，革命的領導者是孫中山。

孫中山(1866—1925)，字逸仙，廣東香山縣(今中山縣)人，中國民主革命的偉大先行者和偉大愛國者。他為中國的獨立、民主、富強奮鬥了一生。孫中山決心推翻清政府，在中國建立一個民主的國家。他首先成立了一個反清革命團體——興中會。1905年，他又聯合其他革命團體，在日本東京創立了中國同盟會，提出了"驅除韃(dá)虜，恢復中華，建立民國，平均地權"的口號。同盟會成立以後，革命者在長江中下游和南方各地，連續發動了一系列武裝起義。經過長期艱苦的努力，1911年10月10日，革命黨人在武昌的起義終於取得了成功，各省革命黨人和反清力量紛紛響應。因為1911年是中國農曆辛亥年，所以這次革命被稱為辛亥革命。1912年1月1日，孫中山在南京就任中華民國臨時大總統。之後，清朝皇帝宣佈退位。但是，後來權力落到了北

武昌起義後成立的湖北軍政府

洋軍閥袁世凱的手中。

辛亥革命推翻了清王朝，結束了中國兩千多年的封建君主制度，建立了中華民國。

生詞

nì chā 逆差	trade deficit		cái pàn 裁判	judgement
ní róng 呢絨	wollen cloth		zhí mín dì 殖民地	colony
jù jué 拒絶	refuse; reject		wán gù 頑固	stubborn; obstinate
zuì è 罪惡	evil; crime		tán 譚	Tan (*surname*)
yā piàn 鴉片	opium		xīn hài gé mìng 辛亥革命	the Revolution of 1911
shōu jiǎo 收繳	take over; confiscate		xiǎng yìng 響應	respond
xiāo huǐ 銷毁	destroy by burning		lín shí 臨時	temporary
jūn jiàn 軍艦	warship; naval vessel		kǎi 凱	triumphant
péi cháng 賠償	compensate			

聽寫

拒絶　軍艦　賠償　裁判　臨時　凱（歌）　頑固　響應

罪惡　殖民地　*逆差　鴉片

比一比

罪：罪惡　受罪　犯罪

響：響應　影響　響聲

賠：賠償　賠款　賠錢

艦（軍艦）　船（小船）

使：使節　使用

鎮：鎮壓　城鎮

殖：殖民地　繁殖

裁：裁判　裁縫

詞語運用

遭受

親愛的媽媽去世了，他遭受了一次沉重的打擊，心情十分悲痛。

忍受

窗外機器的響聲吵得大家上不了課，師生們實在忍受不了了。

賠償

損壞了別人的財物就應該賠償。

反義詞

逆差——順差　　　　拒絕——接受

多音字

ní 呢	ne 呢
ní 呢絨	ne 在哪兒呢

回答問題

1. 鴉片戰爭爆發的原因是什麼?

2. 為什麼說簽訂《南京條約》使中國變成了半殖民地半封建的國家?

3. 什麼革命推翻了清朝? 革命的領導人是誰?

詞語解釋

冒天下之大不韙——做天下人都認為不對的壞事。

舉世無雙——世界上沒有第二個。

合法——符合法律規定。

驅除韃虜——趕走清朝統治者。

閱讀

林則徐虎門銷煙

林則徐（1785—1850），福建省福州人，是中國近代的民族英雄。

公元1839年，清道光皇帝派林則徐去廣東禁煙。林則徐到達廣州後，當衆表示“如鴉片一日未禁絶，本大臣一日不回京”。公元1839年3月16日，林則徐下令收繳外商鴉片。他限外商三天内交出所有鴉片；個人還要出保證書，聲明：以後來船絶不夾帶鴉片。林則徐又在廣東省内下令嚴禁販賣、吸食鴉片，兩個月内捕獲販賣、吸食鴉片者1,600多名，收繳鴉片46萬兩，煙槍4萬多支；收繳外商鴉片2萬多箱，合計1,188噸。

虎門銷煙（人民英雄紀念碑浮雕）

公元1839年6月3日，林則徐在虎門開始銷煙。清兵在虎門海灘高地上，築了兩個長寬各45米的方形大池子，並放入鹽水。先把鴉片過秤後投入水中，再將石灰撒入池中，池水頓時沸騰，直到鴉片全部化盡。虎門銷煙進行了23天。附近居民歡欣鼓舞，紛紛前往觀看這一空前壯舉。

林則徐虎門銷煙，震驚世界。它向全世界表明了中國人禁煙的決心和反抗外國侵略的堅強意志。

生詞

bǎo zhèng shū 保證書	letter of guarantee	zhuàng jǔ 壯舉	magnificent feat
jiā dài 夾帶	carry secretly; smuggle	zhèn jīng 震驚	astound
dùn shí 頓時	immediately	jiān qiáng 堅強	strong
fèi téng 沸騰	boil	yì zhì 意志	will; power
huān xīn gǔ wǔ 歡欣鼓舞	filled with exultation; jubilant		

Lesson 19

Qing（II）

At the end of the 18th century, the United Kingdom suffered great deficit in its Sino-British trade. The British people loved drinking tea and had to import large amounts of tea leaves from China, while its woolen goods and clocks were not well marketed and there was hardly any demand for such products in the Chinese market. Because of this, the United Kingdom used to send envoys to China in the hope of developing the Chinese market via diplomatic measures, only to be refused and rejected by Emperor Qianlong. In order to reverse the trade deficit, the United Kingdom risked everyone's condemnation and started the villainous opium trade. From A.D. 1838, more than 40,000 boxes of opium were sold to China every year, and this caused great damage to the ordinary people as it resulted in the outflow of a large amount of silver. From A.D. 1820 to A.D. 1840, the total value of silver flowing out of China equaled the financial revenue of the Qing government for two years.

At the end of A.D. 1838, the emperor of the Qing Dynasty ordered Lin Zexu to ban opium smoking and trading. The next year, Lin Zexu arrived at Guangzhou and destroyed all confiscated opium in Humen. This episode is known in history as the famous "Destruction of Opium at Humen." In A.D. 1840, the United Kingdom sent warships to invade Guangzhou and Zhejiang, which led to the start of the Opium War. Due to the Qing army's resistance, the British army suffered failure and turned to the north till Tianjin and threatened Beijing. Then the British army went deep through the mouth of the Yangtze River till the Nanjing city. In A.D. 1842, the Qing government was forced to sign the *Nanjing Treaty* with the United Kingdom, the first treaty of inequality in the modern history of China. According to the treaty, China had to compensate the United Kingdom 21 million silver dollars, cede Hong Kong Island, open five trading ports, and grant the United Kingdom unilateral consular jurisdiction. Since then, China became a semi-colonist and semi-feudal society.

After the Opium War, the United Kingdom and France started the Second Opium War in A.D. 1856 in the hope of getting more benefits from China. In A.D. 1860, the British and the French expeditionary forces entered Beijing and set fire on the unprecedented imperial park, the Winter Palace (Yuan Ming Yuan). Emperor Xianfeng of the Qing Dynasty escaped to Chengde and after his death due to illness in A.D. 1861, one of his concubines joined hands with one of his brothers in launching a coup d'état in Beijing and they successfully seized the ruling power. The concubine was later known as Empress Dowager Cixi or the "West Empress Dowager." The period under her reign was the darkest stage of the entire Qing Dynasty. She was stubborn, conservative, and strongly against reforms of any kind. She repressed the farmer uprising of the Taiping Heavenly Kingdom, the Yihetuan Movement, and ordered the killing of heroes from the 100-Day Reform Movement of 1898 including people like Tan Sitong. However, facing the invasion of U.K., France, and Japan, the Qing government at the time could not resist and had no choice but to retreat.

Within 50 years in the late 19th century, the opium trade became legal and the scale of foreign invasions grew, causing increasing severe damages to China. Firstly, Russia forced the Qing government to sign the *Treaty of Aigun*. After the war with France, the *Sino-France New Treaty* was signed. After the Sino-Japanese war, the *Treaty of Shimonoseki* was settled. After the invasion of the Eight Power Allied Force, the *Treaty of 1901* was signed. With all these treaties of inequality, China lost a total territory of 1.5 million square kilometers in the northeast and the northwest, as well as Taiwan, the New Territories of Hong Kong, Dalian, and Qingdao, and had to pay a total indemnity of over one billion *liang* of silver (including interest). China suffered the greatest strike ever in its history and its people could not stand for it. A great revolution was initiated, and the leader of this rebellion was Sun Zhongshan (Sun Yat-Sen).

Sun Zhongshan (1866-1925), also known as Yat-Sen, nicknamed Zhongshan, was born in Xiangshan County (today's Zhongshan County) of Guangdong. He was a great pioneer and patriot of the Chinese democratic revolution. He devoted all his life for the independence, democracy, and prosperity of China. Sun Zhongshan determined to overthrow the Qing government and rebuild it into a democratic country. He firstly established the Revive China Society, a revolutionary group against Qing. In A.D. 1905, he cooperated with other revolutionary groups and founded the Chinese Revolutionary Alliance (*Tongmenghui*) in Tokyo, Japan. This society proposed "to overthrow the Manchu empire, to restore China to the Chinese, to establish a Republic, and to distribute land equally among the people." After the founding of the Chinese Revolutionary Alliance, the revolutionists launched a series of armed revolts in the middle and lower reaches of the Yangtze River and in southern China. Over many years of efforts, the uprising in Wuchang finally succeeded on 10 October 1911. This set off uprisings from other revolutionists and forces against the Qing government in other provinces. According to the traditional Chinese lunar calendar, 1911 is the year of Xinhai (the forty-eighth year in a cycle of 60 years)

and hence the revolution was thus known as the Revolution of Xinhai, or the Revolution of 1911. On 1 January 1912, Sun Zhongshan took the post of the interim president of the Republic of China in Nanjing. The emperor of the Qing Dynasty announced then that he would abdicate his throne but the power was seized later on by a northern warlord, Yuan Shikai.

The Revolution of 1911 overthrew the Qing Dynasty and ended the feudal monarchy which had a long history of more than 2,000 years in China and the Republic of China was founded.

The Destruction of Opium at Humen Led by Lin Zexu

Lin Zexu (1785-1850) who was born in Fuzhou, Fujian Province, was regarded as a national hero in the modern history of China.

In A.D. 1839, Emperor Daoguang of the Qing Dynasty sent Lin Zexu to Guangdong to impose a ban on opium-smoking and the opium trade. When he arrived in Guangzhou, Lin Zexu said to the public that, "I won't go back to Beijing until opium is banned." On 16 March 1839, Lin Zexu ordered to confiscate opium from foreign businessmen and gave them a three-day deadline to hand over all their opium together with a personal statement promising not to transport opium on their boats in the future. Lin Zexu then distributed orders in Guangdong Province that no opium was allowed to be sold and taken. Within the following two months, the local government caught more than 1,600 people selling or taking opium, confiscated 460,000 *liang* of opium and more than 40,000 opium pipes, as well as 20,000 boxes and 1,188 tons of opium from foreign businessmen.

On 3 June 1839, Lin Zexu ordered to destroy all the confiscated opium in Humen. The Qing soldiers dug two square pools of 45 meters long and wide on the highland area of the beach of Humen and then filled the pools with salt water. They weighed the opium and then threw them into the water before spreading lime into the pool. The lime caused the water in the pool to boil till all the opium was melted. It took 23 days to destroy all the opium at Humen. The local people were overjoyed and witnessed the grand view in groups.

The Destruction of Opium at Humen led by Lin Zexu shook the world, as it demonstrated the determination of the Chinese people in banning opium and their strong will in fighting against the foreign invaders.

生字表（繁）

péng bó shù chǒng fēi nài cháo pàn càn yǔn xún
11. 蓬 勃 庶 寵 妃 奈 巢 叛 燦 允 詢

cái yōng jiān qīn lǔ guī xiǔ
12. 財 庸 奸 欽 擄 瑰 朽

qì dǎng fú zhào xiáng fāng qīn chāo
13. 契 黨 俘 召 祥 芳 侵 鈔

chí xiōng xù wù kuà lái yīn yī miǎn diàn
14. 馳 匈 旭 兀 跨 萊 茵 伊 緬 甸

hè jiǎn péng kěn sāng chàng yuè cáo dìng dòu xiāng qí
15. 赫 檢 澎 墾 桑 倡 躍 漕 訂 竇 厢 歧

zhèng bì jiā yù gù yōng yáo shòu xú méi
16. 鄭 碧 嘉 峪 雇 傭 窯 售 徐 煤

huàn cōng xià zhāng
17. 宦 匆 廈 彰

xī qián gá màn jì zhì
18. 熙 乾 噶 曼 祭 致

nì róng jù jiǎo jiàn cháng pàn tán hài kǎi
19. 逆 絨 拒 繳 艦 償 判 譚 亥 凱

共計78個生字

生字表（简）

	péng	bó	shù	chǒng	fēi	nài	cháo	pàn	càn	yǔn	xún	
11.	蓬	勃	庶	宠	妃	奈	巢	叛	灿	允	询	
	cái	yōng	jiān	qīn	lǔ	guī	xiǔ					
12.	财	庸	奸	钦	掳	瑰	朽					
	qì	dǎng	fú	zhào	xiáng	fāng	qīn	chāo				
13.	契	党	俘	召	祥	芳	侵	钞				
	chí	xiōng	xù	wù	kuà	lái	yīn	yī	miǎn	diàn		
14.	驰	匈	旭	兀	跨	莱	茵	伊	缅	甸		
	hè	jiǎn	péng	kěn	sāng	chàng	yuè	cáo	dìng	dòu	xiāng	qí
15.	赫	检	澎	垦	桑	倡	跃	漕	订	窦	厢	歧
	zhèng	bì	jiā	yù	gù	yōng	yáo	shòu	xú	méi		
16.	郑	碧	嘉	峪	雇	佣	窑	售	徐	煤		
	huàn	cōng	xià	zhāng								
17.	宦	匆	厦	彰								
	xī	qián	gá	màn	jì	zhì						
18.	熙	乾	噶	曼	祭	致						
	nì	róng	jù	jiǎo	jiàn	cháng	pàn	tán	hài	kǎi		
19.	逆	绒	拒	缴	舰	偿	判	谭	亥	凯		

共计78个生字

生詞表（繁）

11. péng tó 蓬勃　fù shù 富庶　cì xiù 刺繡　chǒng ài 寵愛　guì fēi 貴妃　fèn nù 憤怒　wú nài 無奈　huáng cháo 黄巢
pàn biàn 叛變　càn làn 燦爛　yǔn xǔ 允許　zōng jiào 宗教　zǐ wǔ xiàn 子午線　ōu yáng xún 歐陽詢　fēng gé 風格

12. jiě chú 解除　jiāo nà 交納　cái zhèng 財政　gǎi gé 改革　dī (lì) xī 低（利）息　bǎo shǒu pài 保守派　hūn yōng 昏庸
jiān chén 奸臣　sòng qīn zōng 宋欽宗　gē dì 割地　lǔ zǒu 擄走　guī bǎo 瑰寶　miáo huì 描繪　bù xiǔ 不朽

13. qì dān 契丹　wéi chí 維持　dǎng xiàng 黨項　fú lǔ 俘虜　běi fá 北伐　zhào huí 召回　wén tiān xiáng 文天祥
qiān gǔ liú fāng 千古流芳　cóng róng 從容　jiù yì 就義　qīn lüè 侵略　yìng yòng 應用　tuī guǎng 推廣　fā xíng 發行
chāo piào 鈔票

14. yóu mù 遊牧　bēn chí 奔馳　hùn luàn 混亂　xiōng yá lì 匈牙利　xù liè wù 旭烈兀　kuà 跨　lái yīn hé 萊茵河
běi bīng yáng 北冰洋　yī lǎng 伊朗　yī lā kè 伊拉克　tǔ ěr qí 土耳其　miǎn diàn 緬甸　bā jī sī tǎn 巴基斯坦

15. hè hè wǔ gōng 赫赫武功　miàn mào 面貌　jiǎn chá 檢（查）　péng hú liè dǎo 澎湖列島　kāi kěn 開墾　sāng 桑　tí chàng 提倡
huó yuè 活躍　jīng lì 經歷　cáo yùn 漕運　zhì dìng 制訂　xì qǔ 戲曲　dòu 竇　xiāng 廂　qí shì 歧視　lǐng xiù 領袖

16. tài jiàn 太監　zhèng 鄭　bù jú 佈局　jīn bì huī huáng 金碧輝煌　jiā yù guān 嘉峪關　duō yú 多餘　gù yōng 雇傭
yáo 窯　chéng zhèn 城鎮　xiāo shòu 銷售　shùn chā 順差　wén xiàn 文獻　xú guāng qǐ 徐光啓　chuán jiào shì 傳教士
cǎi méi 採煤　gōng yì 工藝　wén yì fù xīng 文藝復興

17\. 宦官 huàn guān　皇親國戚 huáng qīn guó qì　財富 cái fù　處境 chǔ jìng　壯大 zhuàng dà　匆忙 cōngmáng　收復 shōu fù

廈門 xià mén　驅逐 qū zhú　荷蘭 hé lán　基地 jī dì　家屬 jiā shǔ　彰化 zhāng huà　治理 zhì lǐ　歸順 guī shùn

18\. 乘機 chéng jī　康熙 kāng xī　簽訂 qiān dìng　劃定 huà dìng　乾隆 qián lóng　準噶爾 zhǔn gá ěr　負擔 fù dān

日耳曼 rì ěr màn　祭孔 jì kǒng　觸及 chù jí　自居 zì jū　覺察 jué chá　民主 mín zhǔ　契約 qì yuē　專制 zhuān zhì

(以)致 yǐ zhì　潮流 cháo liú

19\. 逆差 nì chā　呢絨 ní róng　拒絕 jù jué　罪惡 zuì è　鴉片 yā piàn　收繳 shōu jiǎo　銷毀 xiāo huǐ　軍艦 jūn jiàn

賠償 péi cháng　裁判 cái pàn　殖民地 zhí mín dì　頑固 wán gù　譚 tán　辛亥革命 xīn hài gé mìng　響應 xiǎng ying

臨時 lín shí　凱 kǎi

共計139個生詞

生词表（简）

péng tó　fù shù　cì xiù　chǒng ài　guì fēi　fèn nù　wú nài　huáng cháo
11. 蓬勃　富庶　刺绣　宠爱　贵妃　愤怒　无奈　黄巢

pàn biàn　càn làn　yǔn xǔ　zōng jiào　zǐ wǔ xiàn　xún　fēng gé
叛变　灿烂　允许　宗教　子午线　询　风格

jiě chú　jiāo nà　cái zhèng　gǎi gé　dī lì xī　bǎo shǒu pài　hūn yōng
12. 解除　交纳　财政　改革　低（利）息　保守派　昏庸

jiān chén　sòng qīn zōng　gē dì　lǔ zǒu　guī bǎo　miáo huì　bù xiǔ
奸臣　宋钦宗　割地　掳走　瑰宝　描绘　不朽

qì dān　wéi chí　dǎng xiàng　fú lǔ　běi fá　zhào huí　wén tiān xiáng
13. 契丹　维持　党项　俘虏　北伐　召回　文天祥

qiān gǔ liú fāng　cóng róng　jiù yì　qīn lüè　yìng yòng　tuī guǎng　fā xíng
千古流芳　从容　就义　侵略　应用　推广　发行

chāo piào
钞票

yóu mù　bēn chí　hùn luàn　xiōng yá lì　xù liè wù　kuà　lái yīn hé
14. 游牧　奔驰　混乱　匈牙利　旭烈兀　跨　莱茵河

běi bīng yáng　yī lǎng　yī lā kè　tǔ ěr qí　miǎn diàn　bā jī sī tǎn
北冰洋　伊朗　伊拉克　土耳其　缅甸　巴基斯坦

hè hè wǔ gōng　miàn mào　jiǎn chá　péng hú liè dǎo　kāi kěn　sāng　tí chàng
15. 赫赫武功　面貌　检（查）　澎湖列岛　开垦　桑　提倡

huó yuè　jīng lì　cáo yùn　zhì dìng　xì qǔ　dòu　xiāng　qí shì　lǐng xiù
活跃　经历　漕运　制订　戏曲　窦　厢　歧视　领袖

tài jiàn　zhèng　bù jú　jīn bì huī huáng　jiā yù guān　duō yú　gù yōng
16. 太监　郑　布局　金碧辉煌　嘉峪关　多余　雇佣

yáo　chéng zhèn　xiāo shòu　shùn chā　wén xiàn　xú guāng qǐ　chuán jiào shì
窑　城镇　销售　顺差　文献　徐光启　传教士

cǎi méi　gōng yì　wén yì fù xīng
采煤　工艺　文艺复兴

huàn guān　huáng qīn guó qì　cái fù　chǔ jìng　zhuàng dà　cōngmáng　shōu fù
17. 宦官　皇亲国戚　财富　处境　壮大　匆忙　收复

xià mén　qū zhú　hé lán　jī dì　jiā shǔ　zhāng huà　zhì lǐ　guī shùn
厦门　驱逐　荷兰　基地　家属　彰化　治理　归顺

chéng jī　kāng xī　qiān dìng　huà dìng　qián lóng　zhǔn gá ěr　fù dān
18. 乘机　康熙　签订　划定　乾隆　准噶尔　负担

rì ěr màn　jì kǒng　chù jí　zì jū　jué chá　mín zhǔ　qì yuē　zhuān zhì
日耳曼　祭孔　触及　自居　觉察　民主　契约　专制

yǐ zhì　cháo liú
（以）致　潮流

nì chā　ní róng　jù jué　zuì è　yā piàn　shōu jiǎo　xiāo huǐ　jūn jiàn
19. 逆差　呢绒　拒绝　罪恶　鸦片　收缴　销毁　军舰

péi cháng　cái pàn　zhí mín dì　wán gù　tán　xīn hài gé mìng　xiǎng yìng
赔偿　裁判　殖民地　顽固　谭　辛亥革命　响应

lín shí　kǎi
临时　凯

共计139个生词

中國歷史朝代年表

夏　約公元前21世紀——約公元前17世紀

商　約公元前17世紀——約公元前11世紀

周　**西周**　約公元前11世紀——公元前771年

　　東周　公元前770年——公元前256年

　　　春秋時代　公元前770年——公元前476年

　　　戰國時代　公元前475年——公元前221年

秦　公元前221年——公元前206年

漢　西漢　公元前206年——公元25年

　　東漢　公元25年——公元220年

三国（魏蜀吴）　公元220年——公元280年

西晋　公元265年——公元317年

東晋　十六國　公元317年——公元420年

南北朝　公元420年——公元589年

隋　公元581年——公元618年

唐　公元618年——公元907年

五代十國　公元907年——公元960年

宋　**北宋**　公元960年——公元1127年

　　南宋　公元1127年——公元1279年

遼　公元916年——公元1125年

西夏　公元1038年——公元1227年

金　公元1115年——公元1234年

元　公元1271年——公元1368年

明　公元1368年——公元1644年

清　公元1644年——公元1911 年

王雙雙 編著
Shuangshuang Wang

雙雙中文教材（20）

Chinese Language and Culture Course

練習册

（第二十册 單課）

姓名：______________

年級：______________

第十一課

一 寫生詞

蓬	勃											
富	庶											
寵	愛											
貴	妃											
無	奈											
黃	巢											
叛	變											
燦	爛											
允	許											
歐	陽	詢										

二　組詞

蓬＿＿＿＿	腐＿＿＿＿	奈＿＿＿＿	宗＿＿＿＿
燦＿＿＿＿	叛＿＿＿＿	庶＿＿＿＿	妃＿＿＿＿
寵＿＿＿＿	爆＿＿＿＿	播＿＿＿＿	憤＿＿＿＿

三　選字組詞

無(奈　耐)	(允　充)許	蓬(脖　勃)
(奈　耐)心	(允　充)分	(脖　勃)子

四　根據課文選擇正確答案

1. 唐朝前期,唐是當時世界上最＿＿＿＿＿＿。

　A 衰弱落後的國家　　　　B 富庶、強盛的國家

2. 安史之亂以後,唐朝走向＿＿＿＿＿＿。

　A 衰落　　　　B 蓬勃發展

3. 唐朝末年爆發了＿＿＿＿起義,唐帝國滅亡。

　A 黄巾　　　　B 黄巢

4. 隋唐時期,與中國通商的國家有＿＿＿＿個。

　A 17　　　　B 70 多

5. 在長安、洛陽、廣州等城市,有來自新羅(朝鮮)、____________等國的外國商人和留學生。

A 日本、波斯和東羅馬　　B 波斯、非洲、美洲

6. 唐朝政府平等對待外國人,允許他們在中國居住,和中國人________。

A 通婚　　B 當官

7. 在長安、洛陽這些大城市,有許多外國商人開的________。

A 商店和酒館　　B 街道和圖書館

8. 在__________時期,景教、伊斯蘭教也傳入了中國。

A 秦漢　　B 隋唐　　C 春秋戰國

9. 唐朝是中國詩歌的黃金時代,著名詩人有________。

A 李白和唐僧等　　B 李白、杜甫和白居易等

10. 唐玄宗時,天文學家________測量出了子午線的長度。

A 一行和尚　　B 一行教授

五　造句

1. 無奈______________________________

2. 允許______________________________

六 回答問題

1. 唐朝是中國歷史上很開放的時期,對嗎?請舉例説一説當時開放的情況。

答:______________________________

____

2. 唐代有多少國家和中國通商?

答:______________________________

____

3. 隋唐時期有哪些著名的建築?

答:______________________________

____

4. 唐代漢族和其他民族生活在一起,對文化的發展有什麼好處?

答:______________________________

____

七 根據閱讀材料選擇填空

1. 莫高窟,俗稱千佛洞,位於__________省。

(河北　甘肅)

yá
2. 公元 366 年，一位________在崖壁上建造了第一個佛窟。

（僧人　藝術家）

dūn huáng
3. 敦 煌 莫高窟壁畫有許多________故事。

（景教　佛教）

pí bā
4. “飛天”和“反彈琵琶”等是敦煌________的代表作。

（壁畫　塑像）

5. 莫高窟是一座________的寶庫。

（文化藝術　科學技術）

八　寫一寫《燦爛的隋唐文化》（不少於 200 字）

____

____

____

____

____

____

____

____

九 熟讀課文

第十三課

一 寫生詞

契	丹											
黨	項											
俘	虜											
召	回											
文	天	祥										
侵	略											
鈔	票											
千	古	流	芳									

二 組詞

境________ 維________ 制________ 謀________

應________ 伐________ 鈔________ 俘________

侵________ 芳________________

三 選字組詞

(芳 方)香　　邊(境 鏡)　　維(持 特)

(芳 方)向　　(境 鏡)子　　(持 特)別

(鈔 吵)票　　文天(祥 詳)

爭(鈔 吵)　　(祥 詳)細

四 根據課文選擇正確答案

1. 宋朝當時有三個敵人:____________________。

(戰國 遼國 西夏 金國)

2. 遼是________建立的。(契丹人 女真族)

3. 金國是________建立的。(女真族 契丹人)

4. 宋徽宗的另一個兒子於公元 1127 年在臨安建立________。(南宋 唐朝)

5. 岳飛是宋朝著名的________將領。(抗金 抗日)

6. 忽必烈於公元 1271 年建立________。(漢朝 元朝)

7. ________寫下了"人生自古誰無死,留取丹心照汗青"的詩句。(文天祥 岳飛)

8. 宋朝的＿＿＿＿＿＿＿＿在當時世界上是非常先進的。

（建築業　陶瓷業和造船業）

9. 宋朝出現了世界上最早的＿＿＿＿＿——交子。

（金幣　紙幣）

10. 活字印刷是＿＿＿＿＿時發明的。

（漢朝　秦朝　宋朝）

11. 發明於唐代的火藥到宋代＿＿＿＿＿。

（已廣泛應用　未廣泛應用）

五 造句

1. 順利＿＿＿＿＿＿＿＿＿＿＿＿＿＿＿＿＿＿＿＿

2. 應用＿＿＿＿＿＿＿＿＿＿＿＿＿＿＿＿＿＿＿＿

六 回答問題

1. 契丹人和西夏人怎樣學習漢文化？

答：＿＿＿＿＿＿＿＿＿＿＿＿＿＿＿＿＿＿＿＿＿＿

＿＿＿＿＿＿＿＿＿＿＿＿＿＿＿＿＿＿＿＿＿＿＿＿

＿＿＿＿＿＿＿＿＿＿＿＿＿＿＿＿＿＿＿＿＿＿＿＿

2. 契丹、黨項等民族學習漢文化對民族融合有什麽好處?(選做題)

答:____

____

七 根根據閱讀材料選擇填空

1. 岳飛的軍隊叫"岳家軍",金軍十分________他們。

(害怕　勇敢)

2. 岳飛熱愛祖國,被稱為________。(英雄　將軍)

3. 秦檜(huì)殺害岳飛,________被人唾(tuò)罵。(世代　年代)

八 寫一寫《發達的兩宋文化》(不少於200字)

____

____

____

____

____

____

____

九 熟讀課文

第十五課

一　寫生詞

檢查

開墾

桑

提倡

活躍

漕運

制訂

賓

西廂記

歧視

赫赫武功

澎湖列島

二 組詞

躍________ 倡________ 墾________ 厢________

檢________ 歧________ 領________ 等________

三 選字組詞

(躍 妖)精 激(烈 列) (歧 枝)視

活(躍 妖) 排(烈 列) 樹(歧 枝)

檢(起 查) 提(昌 倡) 車(厢 相)

撿(起 查) 許(昌 倡) (厢 相)信

四 寫出近義詞

開端—— 以往——

五 根據課文選擇正確答案

1. 忽必烈建立的元朝是__________的王朝。

A 蒙古族 B 藏族 C 漢族

2. 忽必烈是一位傑出的皇帝，他保護農業，大力________。

A 推行漢法　　B 推廣蒙古文化

3. 忽必烈提倡以________為主的漢族傳統文化。

A 儒學　　B 天主教　　C 道家

4. 元朝為了保住蒙古貴族的地位，實行________的政策。

A 民族歧視　　B 民族平等

5. 元朝中期，海外貿易空前發達，有許多外國商人和使節________居住在北京。

A 長期　　B 短期

6. 郭守敬是元朝著名的________。

A 文學家　　B 天文學家

7. 元朝的黄道婆改進了當時的________技術。

A 棉紡織　　B 造紙　　C 製茶

8. 元代文化最著名的是________，它是現代戲曲的開端。

A 唐詩　　B 宋詞　　C 元曲

六　造句

激烈 ______________________________

七 詞語解釋

1. 空前——

2. 見聞——

八 回答問題

1. 忽必烈為什麼要重用漢人？

答：____

____

2. 忽必烈怎樣推行漢法？

答：____

____

九 根據閱讀材料選擇填空

1. 馬可·波羅是________人。（意大利　英國）

2. 馬可·波羅是第一個將中國介紹給________的人。

（美洲　歐洲）

3. 馬可·波羅和父親、叔(shū)父三人一路歷經________來到中國。（輕松愉快　千辛萬苦）

4. 忽必烈很________馬可・波羅,派他到國內各地和鄰近國家進行訪問。（依靠　信任）

5. 馬可・波羅和父親、叔父在中國生活了________年。他們想回家鄉威尼斯看看。（十七　七）

6. 馬可・波羅在監獄中把關於________的故事講給一位作家聽,這位作家寫出了著名的《馬可・波羅遊記》。（中國　美國）

十　任選下列一個題目寫一篇短文（不少於200字）

1.《元世祖忽必烈》

2.《馬可・波羅的故事》

____

____

____

____

____

____

____

____

十一　熟讀課文

第十七課

一 寫生詞

宦	官											
匆	忙											
廈	門											
彰	化											

二 組詞

宦________ 戚________ 廈________ 降________

屬________ 驅________ 荷________ 獎________

順________ 壯________ 復________ 富________

匆________ 財________ 基________

三 選字組詞

親(戚　成)　　白(免　兔)　　農(歷　曆)

(戚　成)功　　(免　兔)去　　(歷　曆)史

(驅　區)逐　　(廈　夏)門　　(匆　勿)忙

(驅　區)別　　(廈　夏)天　　請(匆　勿)吸煙

四 寫出近義詞

收復——　　投降——　　宦官——

五 根據課文選擇填空

1. 公元 1661 年鄭成功帶領 2.5 萬名________和幾百艘戰船,向台灣進軍。　(將士　農民)
2. 鄭成功收復台灣後,下令讓幾萬士兵和隨軍家屬________。　(練兵　開荒種田)
3. 鄭成功祖孫三代治理台灣________年。(22　40)
4. 鄭氏三代的治理在台灣歷史上是一個重要的開發和發展時期,稱為"________"。　(明鄭時代　明清時代)

六 根據課文選擇正確答案

1. 明朝中後期,宦官專權,政治＿＿＿＿,皇親國戚佔有大量土地和財富。

   A 開放　　B 腐敗

2. 明末農民起義軍的領袖＿＿＿＿帶領起義軍攻入北京,明朝滅亡。

   A 鄭成功　　B 李自成

3. 明朝大將吳三桂投降＿＿＿＿,聯合清軍一起攻打起義軍。

   A 清軍　　B 宋軍

4. 清軍佔領北京,並把首都遷到＿＿＿＿,開始了對全國的統治。

   A 北京　　B 天津

5. 鄭成功是抗清名將,也是收復＿＿＿＿的民族英雄。

   A 台灣　　B 河北

6. 公元 1662 年,鄭成功驅逐了＿＿＿＿,收回了台灣,以台灣為抗清的基地。

   A 西班牙人　　B 荷蘭人　　C 英國人

7. 公元1683年，清政府派軍進攻台灣，鄭克塽(shuǎng)歸順。自此台灣在清政府直接統治下，屬＿＿＿＿省。

A 福建　　B 廣東

七 回答問題

1. 鄭成功對台灣有什麼貢獻？

答：＿＿＿＿＿＿＿＿＿＿＿＿＿＿＿＿＿＿＿＿＿＿＿＿

＿＿＿＿＿＿＿＿＿＿＿＿＿＿＿＿＿＿＿＿＿＿＿＿＿＿

2. 根據閱讀材料談一談為什麼利瑪(mǎ)竇得到了中國人的信任和友誼(yì)。

答：＿＿＿＿＿＿＿＿＿＿＿＿＿＿＿＿＿＿＿＿＿＿＿＿

＿＿＿＿＿＿＿＿＿＿＿＿＿＿＿＿＿＿＿＿＿＿＿＿＿＿

＿＿＿＿＿＿＿＿＿＿＿＿＿＿＿＿＿＿＿＿＿＿＿＿＿＿

八 根據閱讀材料選擇填空

1. 16世紀，一些歐洲天主教教士來中國＿＿＿＿，其中最有名的是利瑪竇。　（傳教　經商　打仗）

2. 利瑪竇是________人,耶穌會教士。1582年到中國傳教。他建立了中國內地的第一座天主教堂。

(意大利　德國)

3. 利瑪竇努力學習漢語,精通“四書五經”,________中國文化,得到了中國人的信任和友誼。(尊重　厭煩)

4. 利瑪竇還將西方的________、三角學、西方樂器等介紹給中國人。(佛學　幾何學)

5. 利瑪竇把中國經典“四書”、“五經”、《道德經》等譯成拉丁文,介紹到歐洲,成為第一個把________介紹給西方的人。(孔子和儒家思想　孫子兵法)

九　任選下列一個題目寫一篇短文(不少於200字)

1.《民族英雄鄭成功》

2.《利瑪竇的故事》

____

____

____

____

____

十 熟讀課文

第十九課

一 寫生詞

逆	差											
呢	絨											
拒	絶											
收	繳											
軍	艦											
賠	償											
裁	判											
譚												
凱												
辛	亥	革	命									

二 組詞

凱______ 絶______ 鴉______ 艦______

頑______ 償______ 罪______ 殖______

三 選字組詞

(賠 倍)款 軍(艦 船) (頑 玩)固

一(賠 倍) 木(艦 船) (頑 玩)具

(殖 值)民地 (裁 栽)判 賠(嘗 償)

價(殖 值) (裁 栽)種 (嘗 償)試

四 寫出反義詞

逆差—— 拒絶——

五 根據課文選擇正確答案

1. 18 世紀末,英國從中國進口大量茶葉,在中英貿易中,英國一直有很大的______。

A 逆差 B 順差

2. 英國想以外交手段打開中國市場,但是被乾隆皇帝________了。

A 同意　　　　B 拒絶

3. 為了改變貿易逆差,英國居然開始了罪惡的________貿易。

A 鴉片　　　　B 茶葉　　　　C 瓷器

4. 到了 1838 年,每年有________鴉片賣到中國。

A 四百多箱　　　　B 四千多箱　　　　C 四萬多箱

5. 清朝皇帝命令林則徐禁煙。林則徐在虎門將收繳的鴉片全部銷毀,這就是歷史上著名的"________"。

A 鴉片戰爭　　　　B 虎門銷煙

6. 1840 年,英國派軍艦入侵中國,發動了"________"。

A 中法戰爭　　　　B 鴉片戰爭

7. 1842 年,清政府被迫同英國簽訂了中國近代史上第一個________——《南京條約》。

A 不平等條約　　　　B 平等條約

8. 簽訂《南京條約》以後的中國淪為________社會。

A 殖民地　　　　B 半殖民地半封建

9. 1911 年,________領導的辛亥革命推翻了清帝國。

A 林則徐　　　　B 孫中山

10. 辛亥革命推翻了________王朝,建立了中華民國。

A 明　　　　B 清

六 造句

1. 忍受________________________________

2. 拒絕________________________________

七 詞語解釋

1. 冒天下之大不韙(wěi)——

2. 舉世無雙——

八 回答問題

1. 鴉片戰爭爆發的原因是什麼?

答:________________________________

____

____

2. 為什麼説簽訂《南京條約》使中國變為半殖民地半封建的國家?

答:______

______

______

3. 什麼革命推翻了清朝? 革命的領導人是誰?

答:______

______

九 根據閱讀材料判斷對錯

1. 清朝皇帝派林則徐去廣西禁煙。 ____對 ____錯

2. 林則徐下令限外商5天内交出所有鴉片。 ____對 ____錯

3. 林則徐還下令外商個人出保證書,聲明:以後來船絶不夾帶鴉片。 ____對 ____錯

4. 林則徐又在廣東省内,下令嚴禁販賣、吸食鴉片。 ____對 ____錯

5. 兩個月内,林則徐收繳外商鴉片2萬多箱。 ____對 ____錯

十　寫一寫《鴉片戰爭和南京條約》(不少於200字)

十一　熟讀課文

第十一課聽寫

第十三課聽寫

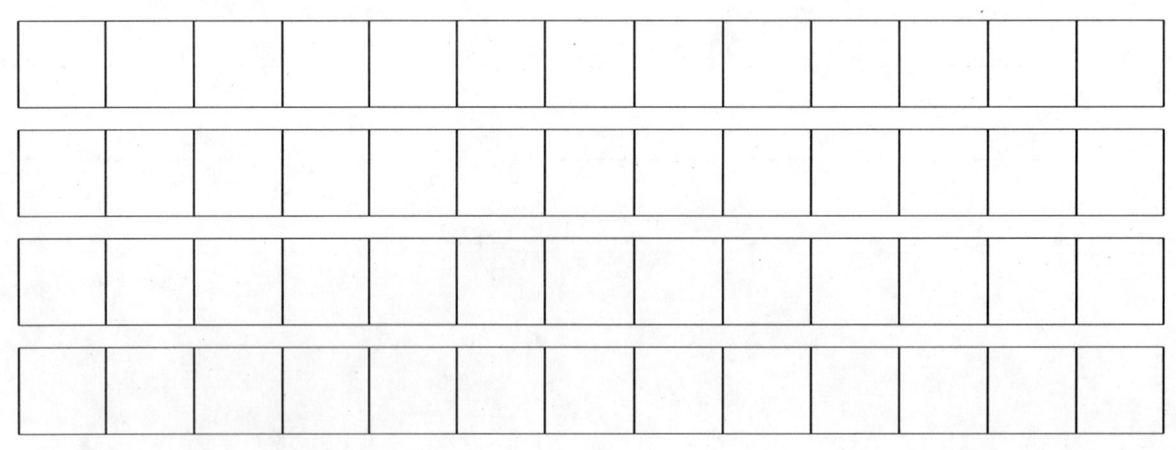

第十五課聽寫

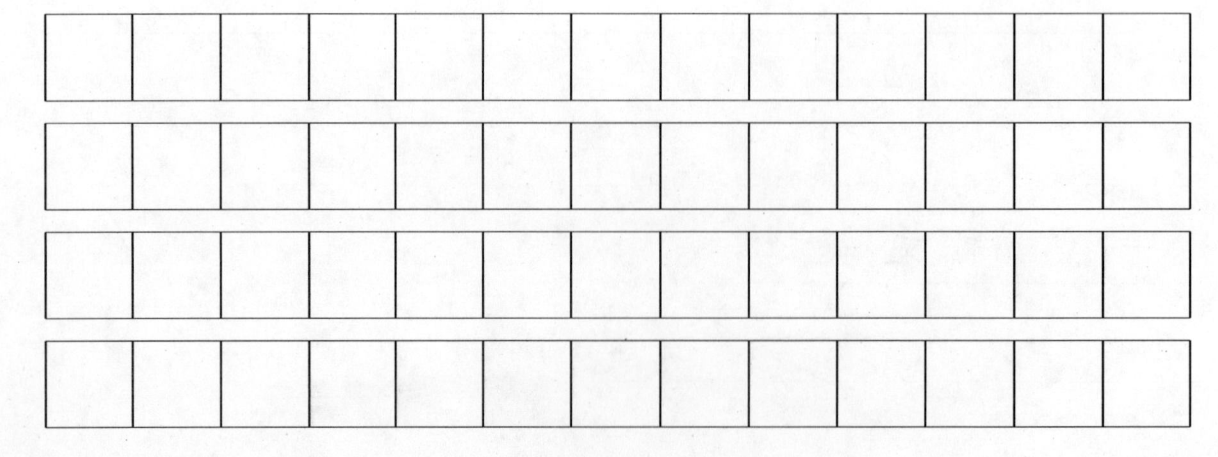

第十七課聽寫

第十九課聽寫

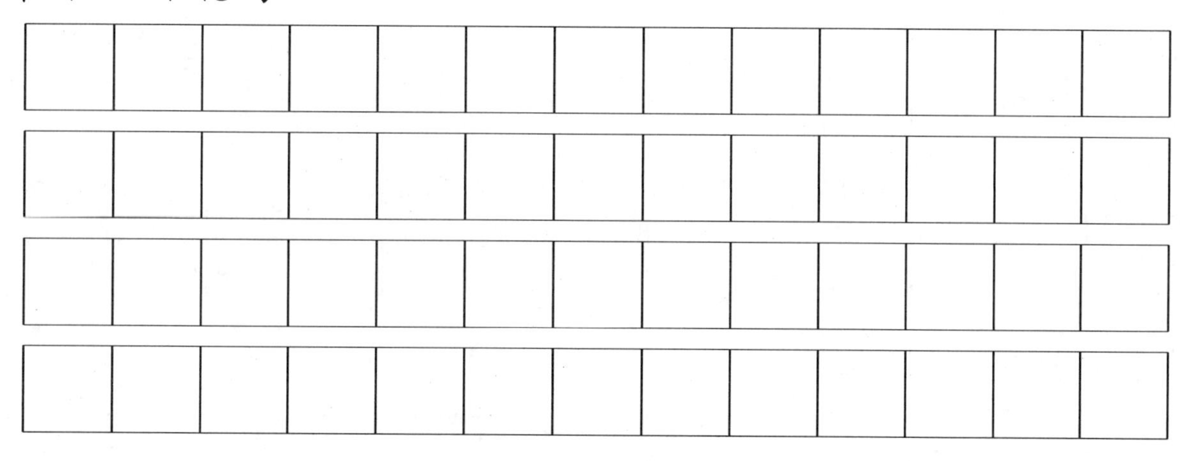

王雙雙 編著
Shuangshuang Wang

雙雙中文教材（20）

Chinese Language and Culture Course

練 習 冊

（第二十册 雙課）

姓名：______________________

年級：______________________

第十二課

一 寫生詞

財	政											
昏	庸											
奸	臣											
宋	欽	宗										
擄	走											
瑰	寶											
不	朽											

二 組詞

宴________ 納________ 財________ 貸________

割________ 賠________ 瑰________ 朽________

罷________ 革________ 利________

三 選字組詞

(割 害)草 棉(幣 布)

(割 害)怕 錢(幣 布)

四 根據課文選擇正確答案

1. 唐朝滅亡後,中國又分裂成很多小國,歷史上把這一時期總稱為"______"。

A 五代十國 B 十國

2. 公元960年,趙匡胤(kuāng yìn)建立______,史稱北宋。

A 宋朝 B 漢朝 C 唐朝

3. ______王安石在皇帝的支持下開始變法。

A 將軍 B 改革家 C 太子

4. 王安石推行新法,最後______。

A 失敗了 B 成功了

5. 北宋被______滅亡。

A 遼國 B 金國 C 西夏

6. 北宋時,雖然戰亂不斷,但南方比較______。

A 安靜 B 安寧 C 安心

7. 北宋時，________有明顯的進步。

A 文學藝術　　　　B 軍事　　　　C 科學技術

五 造句

結束________________________________

六 回答問題

1. 王安石變法的主要內容是什麼？

答：________________________________

____

____

2. "萬般皆下品，唯有讀書高"的觀念和科舉制度有沒有關係？

答：________________________________

____

七 根據閱讀材料選擇填空

1. 北宋時，________發達，是當時世界上的商業大國。

（商業　藝術）

2. 宋朝,在一些港口和交通要道出現了許多________。

(鄉村　城鎮)

3. 北宋的都城有居民________户。　(20 萬　10 萬)

4. 北宋都城内________有數不清的店鋪(pù)、酒樓、飯館。

(大街小巷　廣場)

5. 北宋都城還有娛(yú)樂場所,那裏有戲曲、雜技和________表演。　(武術　電影)

6.《清明上河圖》是宋朝畫家________的作品。

(張擇端　李白)

7.《清明上河圖》畫的是汴(biàn)京________的情景。

(真實生活　神仙)

八　根據閱讀材料選詞填空(把詞語寫在空白處)

人口　城鎮　商業　情景　畫卷　生活

繁華的______　發達的______　流動的______

真實的______　長長的______　熱鬧的______

九 寫一寫《清明上河圖》(不少於200字)

____

____

____

____

____

____

____

____

____

____

十 熟讀課文

第十四課

一 寫生詞

奔	馳											
匈	牙	利										
旭	烈	兀										
跨												
萊	茵	河										
伊	朗											
伊	拉	克										
緬	甸											

二 組詞

牧________ 尚________ 混________ 率________

征________ 續________ 馳________ 匈________

機________ 濱________ 佔________ 括________

三 選字組詞

(匈 胸)牙利　　(跨 誇)越　　緬(句 甸)

(匈 胸)有成竹　　(跨 誇)獎　　(句 甸)子

(佔 站)領　　土(耳 而)其

(佔 站)立　　(耳 而)且

四 根據課文選擇正確答案

1. 蒙古族是生活在蒙古草原上的________民族。

   A 遊牧　　B 農業　　C 商業

2. 成吉思汗的名字是________。

   A 忽必烈　　B 鐵木真

3. 成吉思汗和他的子孫建立了________的蒙古大帝國。

   A 黄河流域　　B 地跨歐亞　　C 歐洲

4. 成吉思汗的孫子忽必烈建立了________,他就是元世祖。

   A 元朝　　B 宋朝

5. 元朝的首都是今天的________。

   A 南京　　B 北京　　C 上海

五 造句

本領______________________________

六 詞語解釋

1. 尚武——

2. 吃苦——

3. 絶好——

七 回答問題

1. 蒙古強大起來的原因是什麼?

答:______________________________

____

____

____

2. 根據閱讀材料簡述中西交通的歷史。

答:______________________________

____

____

____

八 根據閱讀材料判斷對錯

1. 中國對外交通,開始於漢代的絲綢之路。

____對 ____錯

2. 隋唐時期,對外交通除了陸路還有海路。

____對 ____錯

3. 宋代陸路交通中斷,但海路貿易繁榮。 ____對 ____錯

4. 元帝國橫跨歐亞,使世界大通。 ____對 ____錯

5. 元代,東西文化互相傳播。 ____對 ____錯

6. 元政府在長一萬多里的交通大道上建了很多驛站。 ____對 ____錯

7. 元朝,海運事業特別發達。 ____對 ____錯

九 寫一寫《元代的中西交通》(不少於200字)

____

____

____

____

____

____

十 熟讀課文

第十六課

一 寫生詞

鄭	成	功										
嘉	峪	關										
雇	傭											
窯												
銷	售											
徐	光	啓										
採	煤											
金	碧	輝	煌									

二 組詞

啓________　　銷________　　鎮________　　煤________

雇________　　途________　　余________　　碧________

三 選字組詞

(啓　起)發　　(銷　消)售　　金(壁　碧)輝煌

(啓　起)來　　(銷　消)息　　牆(壁　碧)

四 根據課文選擇填空

1. 明朝手工業和商業發達,絲綢和________十分精美。
(青花瓷　棉布)

2. 中國瓷器和絲綢出口到歐洲和美洲,換取了大量的________。
(黄金　白銀)

3.《本草綱目》是一部藥物學巨著,是當時世界上内容最豐富、最詳細的藥物學________。　(文獻　字典)

4.《農政全書》是徐光啓寫的一部________百科全書。
(農業　工業)

5. 徐光啓和意大利傳教士利瑪(mǎ)竇翻譯了中國歷史上第一部科技譯著________。　(《聖經》　《幾何原本》)

6.《天工開物》是________編寫的。(宋應星　徐光啓)

7.《天工開物》被稱為“中國 17 世紀的________”。

（古典小說　詩詞　工藝百科全書）

8. 著名的長篇小說《三國演義》、《水滸(hǔ)傳》和《西遊記》等都寫於________。　（宋代　明代　唐代）

五　根據課文選擇正確答案

1. 公元 1402 年，燕(yān)王朱棣(dì)趕走建文帝，自己做了皇帝，並把首都遷到了________。

A 上海　B 北京　C 天津

2. 北京成為明朝的首都以後，一直是中國________的中心。

A 商業　B 政治、經濟和文化　C 藝術

3. 北京的皇宮金碧輝煌，是現今世界上________古代宮殿建築群。

A 最美麗的　B 最大、保留最完整的

4. 明朝前期是一個繁榮開放的國家。明朝中後期中國開始________。

A 衰落　B 發達

六 造句

1. 多餘________________

2. 沿途________________

七 詞語解釋

1. 金碧輝煌——

2. 胸懷大志——

八 回答問題

明朝的科學家寫出的三部科學巨著是哪三部書?

答:________________

____

九 根據閱讀材料選擇填空

1. 明成祖是一位思想比較________的皇帝,他派太監鄭和率船隊出使西洋。 (開放 開朗 封閉)

2. 公元 1405 年農曆六月的一天,鄭和帶領________揚帆南下。 (船隊 商隊)

3. 明朝前期,中國的紡織、製瓷、造船、航海業都處在世界________地位。 (落後　領先)

4. 鄭和原來姓馬,________人。公元 1371 年出生在雲南。 (漢族　回族)

5. 鄭和第一次下西洋,他的船隊共有________人,有水手、官兵、工匠、醫生、翻譯等。船隊之大,是當時世界上獨一無二的。 (2.7 萬　5,000)

6. 鄭和的寶船長約 138 米,寬 56 米,可容納________人,是當時世界上最大的海船 。 (1,000　500　100)

7. 鄭和七次下西洋,他的船隊到過亞洲和非洲的________多個國家和地區。 (30　20)

十　任選下列一個題目寫一篇短文(不少於 200 字)

1.《明朝的瓷器和絲綢的生產情況》

2.《鄭和下西洋》

____

____

____

____

十一 熟讀課文

第十八課

一 寫生詞

康	熙											
乾	隆											
準	噶	爾										
日	耳	曼										
祭	孔											
以	致											

二 組詞

負________ 居________ 察________ 證________

倡________ 簽________ 致________ 乘________

曼________ 潮________ 觸________ 徒________

三 選字組詞

(擔　但)是　　(提　題)目　　覺(查　察)

負(擔　但)　　(提　題)倡　　檢(查　察)

獎(厲　勵)　　(潮　朝)流

(厲　勵)害　　(潮　朝)鮮

四 根據課文選擇正確答案

1. 清朝是中國封建社會最後一個朝代,是由________建立的。

   A 蒙古族　　B 滿族　　C 漢族

2. 康熙皇帝於公元 1683 年出兵統一了________。

   A 海南　　B 台灣

3. 乾隆皇帝注意發展邊疆經濟文化,鞏固了中國________國家的統一。

   A 多民族　　B 單一民族

4. 從康熙到乾隆三朝，國家穩定，社會繁榮，被稱為“________”。

A 大唐盛世　　B 康乾盛世

5. 清王朝盲目自大，並未覺察歐洲正發生著________的變化。

A 翻天覆地　　B 反反復復

6. 早在 1582 年，意大利傳教士利瑪竇等已來到中國________。

A 傳教　　B 經商

7. 傳教士來到中國，帶來了西方的科學知識。同時，他們也學習中國的________。

A 儒學、佛學　　B 祭孔祭祖

8. 法國、美國建立了民主政權，人民用________治理自己的國家。

A 彩票　　B 選票

9. 大清國文化上提封建禮教，大興________。

A 文字獄　　B 監獄

10. 清政府閉關自守，使中國遠遠________於世界的先進潮流。

A 落後　　B 趕上

五 造句

1. 自大________________

2. 乘機________________

六 回答問題

1. "康乾盛世"的同一時期,歐洲發生了什麼變化?

答:________________

____

____

____

____

2. 清政府覺察到歐洲的巨大變化了嗎? 它採取了什麼樣的做法? 造成了什麼樣的後果?

答:________________

____

____

____

七 根據閱讀材料選擇填空

1. 清朝的文化思想，________儒家禮教，打壓反清言行和文字。 （提倡 打壓）
2. 康乾時期，由官方組織大批________編寫了《四庫全書》和《康熙字典》等許多書籍。 （學者 醫生）
3. 《四庫全書》由乾隆皇帝親自主持，是封建社會________修訂的最大叢書。 （民間 官方）
4. 《四庫全書》編成後，抄成七份，分別藏於北京故宮和江浙等地的藏書樓中。其中江浙藏書樓對公衆開放，供各地文人________。 （買賣 查閱）

八 寫一寫《清朝落後於歐美國家的原因》（不少於200字）

九 熟讀課文

第十二課聽寫

第十四課聽寫

第十六課聽寫

第十八課聽寫
